THE MEDITERRANEAN SLOW COOKER
COOKBOOK

8/12

THE MEDITERRANEAN SLOW COOKER COOKBOOK

by DIANE PHILLIPS

Photographs by Tara Donne

CHRONICLE BOOKS

SAN FRANCISCO

Library of Congress Cataloging-in-Publication Data available.

ISBN 978-1-4521-0300-6

Manufactured in China

Designed by Supriya Kalidas

Food styling by Mariana Velasquez

Prop styling by Pam Morris

The photographer wishes to thank Kyle Acebo

Barilla is a registered trademark of Barilla G.E.R.F. LLI-Societa Per Azioni; Best Foods is a registered trademark of CPC International Inc.; D'Artagnan is a registered trademark of D'Artagnan Inc., Hellman's is a registered trademark of CPC International Inc.; McDonald's is a registered trademark of McDonald's Corporation; Mayan Sweets is a registered trademark of Keystone Fruit Marketing Inc.; More Than Gourmet is a registered trademark of More Than Gourmet Inc.; Old Bay Seasoning is a registered trademark of Old Bay Inc.; Provimi is a registered trademark of Provimi Foods Inc.; Superior Touch Better Than Bouillon is a registered trademark of Superior Quality Foods, Inc.

10 9 8 7 6 5 4 3 2 1

Chronicle Books LLC

680 Second Street

San Francisco, California 94107

www.chroniclebooks.com

*Alla famiglia di Angelini—Roberto, Daniela, Irene, Luca, e Carlo—
con la gratitudine per tutto, e per la loro ospitalità graziosa
[To the Angelini Family—Roberto, Daniela, Irene, Luca, and Carlo—
with gratitude to you all, and for your gracious hospitality]*

ACKNOWLEDGMENTS

As I wrote this book, I was so grateful for the people in my life, who have encouraged and enabled me to follow my passion. They are my superheroes, and I am overwhelmed by their love and support.

I know that this book would not have been possible without the support of my friend and agent Susan Ginsburg, who like any good girlfriend gives you the advice you need and keeps cheering you on; I'm grateful to have Susan in my corner as my agent because she can leap tall buildings in a single bound, but I'm more grateful for her lasting friendship, which is precious.

I'm so grateful to Bill LeBlond for bringing me into the Chronicle family and for his confidence in me and this book. My editor Amy Treadwell's patience, and her generosity for once more blessing me with Deborah Kops as my copy editor, puts her and Bill in the Super Power Rangers category, along with the rest of the gang at Chronicle; David Hawk, Peter Perez, designer Supriya Kalidas, photographer Tara Donne, managing editor Doug Ogan, and production manager Tera Killip.

At home, I can't think of having a better partner to test recipes on than my husband, Chuck; many times that I'm away, he will be left at home eating leftover test recipes, and I'm grateful for all the support he has given to this crazy path I've traveled. Our children, Carrie, Eric, and Ryan, along with our granddaughter, Poppy, are enthusiastic tasters and supporters, and I've always thought of them as the Incredibles, because there is nothing they can't do!

On the road, I'm very grateful to all the cooking schools, their staff, and students who welcome me and let me play in their kitchens; although the hours are long, the rewards are the friendships I've made, that continue to strengthen with each year. It's a privilege to work with each one of you and to know your students.

The industry professionals who gave me the latest (and greatest) machines to test with were invaluable sources of support and I'm grateful to George Bearden and the people at Breville, as well as Dan Kulp at Rachel Litner Associates and Mary Rodgers at Cuisinart for the use of their new multi-machine.

My love for Italy and the Mediterranean sparked the idea for this book; having an adopted family in a small Umbrian hill town has opened our lives and our hearts in ways I can't even explain, but I would be remiss for not saying *Grazie!* to the family I've dedicated this book to. Their hospitality, generosity, and love know no bounds; I often tell people I know nothing about hospitality compared to *la famiglia Angelini*. So, *grazie mille*, Daniela, Roberto, Irene, Luca, and Carlo for teaching us what it means to be family.

Lastly, thank you to you, dear reader, for buying this book and bringing me into your kitchen; as you cook these recipes, let me know how you are doing by joining me online at my website, www.dianephillips.com, or at my blog, www.cucinadivina.blogspot.com.

And now, let's celebrate at the table together!

Contents

INTRODUCTION

The Mediterranean region produces some of the most varied cuisines on the planet—from Málaga, Spain, to Istanbul, Turkey, to Tunis, Tunisia. And many of the foods from this part of the world rely on a slow-cooked method to bring out the flavors of the ingredients and produce meltingly tender dishes.

Slow cooking has been around for thousands of years. One of the earliest slow cookers was a cauldronlike pot used by Cro-Magnon men and women in southwestern France. In modern times, enameled cast-iron Dutch ovens have been used for braising, hammered-steel and copper stockpots for making soups, and conical tagines for making stews. Today's modern and sleek new electric slow cookers are great for making all sorts of dishes, and they do their job off the stove top. A slow-cooked meal has been a comfort food for the ages, satisfying and soothing the soul.

The Portuguese, with their love of the sea and its bounty, prepare seafood in myriad ways; for example, they slow-cook whole fish or fillets on the stove top with potatoes and saffron, and they make enormous pots of seafood stew. Spaniards are famous for their paella, flavored with saffron, pork products, and salt cod. Moving along the northern Mediterranean coastline, we reach France, with its slow-cooked beef stews in red wine, and its famous seafood stew, bouillabaisse. Italian slow-cooked foods range from minestrone, a thick vegetable soup, to porchetta, a stuffed rolled pork shoulder cooked for hours until it falls apart in juicy, tender, rosemary-scented chunks. Greece and Turkey present a variety of slow-cooked foods, from lamb flavored with lemon and rosemary to eggplant dishes. Syria, Lebanon, Egypt, Tunisia, and the entire North African Mediterranean coast boast aromatic and flavorful cuisines, often with ancient roots. A palate of herbs and spices defines their culinary cultures. The slow-cooked dishes of the Mediterranean, served from home and restaurant kitchens, are truly as varied as the region's terrain.

An electric slow cooker in your kitchen can bring the Mediterranean into your home. When you want to make something different and special to serve to family and friends, this book will be your go-to source for great recipes. They reflect a more sophisticated approach to the slow cooker, requiring a few more ingredients, and maybe a few new flavor combinations for you to enjoy, instead of the meat and potatoes you might dump in your machine before running off to work.

Why use the slow cooker? I'm asked this question time and again, and the answer is quite simple. I don't have to baby it along on the stove top or in the oven. I can literally set it and forget it until it is done. With a programmable slow cooker, the food is automatically switched to the warm setting after cooking for the allotted amount of time. I can leave the house, go about my business, and return to a perfectly cooked dinner—no worries about overcooked or burned dishes. Another great benefit of using the slow cooker is that unlike the heat on a stove top or in an oven, the heat in a slow cooker is constant, so all the ingredients cook at the same temperature. Slow cookers are energy efficient, too, using only as much electricity as a 75-watt lightbulb.

Included here are tagines; tender lamb cooked in a variety of ways; classics like Veal Osso Buco (page 69), an Old-Fashioned French Beef Stew (page 56), and Paella Valenciana; seafood with many different herb and spice combinations; Greek Pastitsio (page 128); layered eggplant dishes; and game hens stuffed with savory and aromatic rice in the style of the Egyptian kings (see page 169). There are also accompaniments such as rich legume and rice side dishes, Couscous (page 142), Simple Pita Bread (page 143), and sauces to complement the main dishes.

When you use a slow cooker as your low and slow oven, an elegant dinner for friends can be a reality any night of the week. Or you can cook up a delicious Sunday supper for your family using any of these mouthwatering recipes. You'll learn streamlined techniques for getting these scrumptious dishes to the table, full of fresh flavors. And as we travel around the Mediterranean, sampling its varied and bountiful foods, I'll also include a bit of history.

Where Are We?

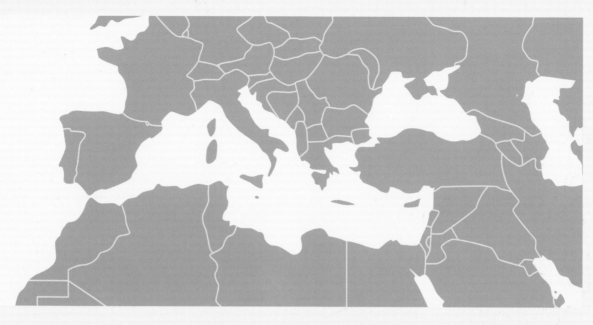

Each country possesses a rich bounty of delicious ingredients for the Mediterranean table: aromatic spices and glistening fresh seafood in the markets of Marrakech, pungent sheep's and goat's milk cheeses on rural Greek farms, truffles in the Dordogne region of France, spring lambs on the salt marshes of France, wild boar in Tuscany, fields of wild oregano in Sicily, and vineyards heavy with grapes throughout the region. Lying roughly between the thirtieth and fortieth parallels of latitude, the Mediterranean enjoys a climate that is generally mild, giving crops in most of the region a long growing season.

History gives us clues about the development of the cuisines of the Mediterranean. European explorers would bring back spices and foods from their travels to Asia in the East and the New World in the West, introducing them into their native countries. Conquering armies from Rome, France, Spain, and Britain brought their own foods and cooking techniques with them, leaving permanent marks on the cuisines of their Mediterranean neighbors. Today, although you will find McDonald's in Marrakech and KFC in Jerusalem, the traditional flavors of the cities' native cuisines are still apparent as you walk through the markets, inhaling the aromas of local spices, produce, meats, cheeses, and seafood. In many places small refrigerators, or none at all, make it necessary for people to shop daily for ingredients. For others, shopping frequently at local markets for the freshest ingredients is a way of life.

Many authors have written exhaustively about the Mediterranean diet, which is now recognized as an "intangible cultural heritage" in Italy by the United Nations Educational, Scientific, and Cultural Organization (UNESCO). It is a way of life and a way of eating, which the Italians call *la cucina genuina* or *la cucina povera* ("genuine cuisine" or "cuisine of the poor"). This is the diet of those who work the land, and feed themselves using seasonal ingredients grown in their small plots outside the kitchen. This is the original back-to-basics cuisine! So come discover some of the most diverse and delicious foods you will ever serve out of your slow cooker; be transported to the Mediterranean, experiencing the tastes of this dynamic part of the world.

Mediterranean Flavors

There are many cookbooks that explore Mediterranean cooking in all its complexity, but I like to keep it simple for the home cook. Although each country that borders the Mediterranean takes pride in its own dishes, they share many ingredients. The following is a simple list of flavors that are the essence of Mediterranean cooking. We could debate this subject forever, but for this book, and these recipes, these items will be essential for a Mediterranean pantry, and you should be able to purchase them without a problem at any full-service grocery store.

SALT	salt, anchovies, prosciutto, capers, olives, roasted salted nuts, some cheeses
ACID	citrus zest and juice, vinegar, wine, tomatoes
SMOKE	smoked paprika, cumin, pancetta, lardons, smoked meats
HEAT	hot chiles, red pepper flakes, spicy sausage
AROMATIC	cinnamon, turmeric, cardamom, coriander, saffron, fennel, paprika, allspice, nutmeg, garlic, onion, ginger
SWEET	sugar, dried fruits, pomegranate, sweet potatoes, carrots, butternut squash, pumpkin
PUNGENT	garlic, onion, ginger, turmeric

A good balance of flavors is the key to making delicious slow-cooked Mediterranean dishes. Since the flavors in these dishes have a long, slow simmer together, it is important that they complement one another, rather than fight for supremacy. Knowing how to combine flavors will help you to prepare balanced dishes in your slow cooker.

When adding salt to a dish, balance it with sweet or aromatics, such as sweet butternut squash with salty prosciutto. Smoke is balanced with aromatics or sweet flavors, and heat is balanced with aromatics. Aromatics and pungent flavors can be balanced with any of the other flavors, while sweet should be balanced with salt, acid, smoke, or aromatics. Acidic ingredients are always balanced by the addition of salt.

The French word *terroir*, meaning "soil," was originally used to describe the way the soil and climate of a particular place affect the taste and aroma of its wines. For example, wines from one region may have a mineral smell and a crisp finish owing to the soil that the grapes are grown in. But today *terroir* means more than that in the Mediterranean. The earth and its components of soil, minerals, water, as well as the climate affect all the foods in the marketplace, and on the table. For example, olive oil in one region may be buttery, while another olive oil leaves a strong peppery aftertaste in the back of your throat. The contrast between the two is a result of different soil, climate, and methods of harvesting in each region. Cheese is flavored by the diet of the cows, sheep, or goats whose milk produces the cheese. And the grasses they eat vary from one region to the next as a result of the differing content of the soil. *Terroir* influences every aspect of Mediterranean cuisine.

Regional preferences have a great influence on Mediterranean cooking, too. In Greece, yogurt and strong sheep's milk cheeses are found in kitchens. Northern Italians like to cook with butter, cow's milk cheeses, and cream, while southern Italians use olive oil rather than butter, and they flavor their food with sharp sheep's milk cheeses. Many regions pride themselves on their smoked and cured meats; Serrano ham in Spain, prosciutto in Italy, and luxurious French hams all contribute smoke or salt to various dishes. Lamb and goat are particular favorites in the southern Mediterranean and along the North African coast, and so are small game hens, guinea fowl, and chicken. Since many Mediterranean countries are poor, with populations that cannot afford meat in their daily diet, beans and legumes provide the protein in many dishes. Lentil and rice dishes abound, too; I could write a whole chapter on those alone. Meats and poultry, when used, generally stay in the background, and in some cases religious dietary laws govern which meats are common to the cuisine.

Using Your Slow Cooker

Using an electric slow cooker to make traditional foods from the Mediterranean is what I call a no-brainer; the ingredients are sautéed and then added to the cooker for a long and slow simmer. This isn't rocket science, or even culinary science. It is simple food cooked in a way that is ages old, using electricity instead of a fire.

All the recipes in this book were tested in 5-, 6-, and 7-qt/4.5-, 5.5-, and 6.5-L slow cookers. If you have one of these sizes, or even a 4-qt/3.5-L, you can make any dish. Some cooking times are loose; something may cook for 4 to 5 hours until tender, not precisely 4½ hours. For maximum success, below are a few more tips to keep in mind.

TIPS FOR SLOW COOKING

❋ Never add water to slow cooker dishes; instead add broth, stock, soup bases, fruit juices, or wine. Water will not add flavor, whereas a broth or stock or other flavorful liquid will season the finished sauce. If you already have a slow cooker you know it creates a steam bath once it gets up to temperature. Steam is created and held in the pot, and the ingredients actually sweat as they cook, adding more liquid. Some cuts of meat, like pork shoulder and chuck roast, will give you up to 4 cups/960 ml of extra liquid as they cook. By adding a small amount of liquid (and sometimes none at all), you will end up with a more concentrated, flavorful sauce to serve with your dish. To that end, in some recipes I recommend that you use a soup base like Superior Touch Better Than Bouillon or a demi-glace concentrate like Provimi or More Than Gourmet, which are readily available in supermarkets or gourmet stores. If you don't want to use a soup base, boiling the sauce on the stove top to reduce the liquid that has collected in your slow cooker (after cooking) will help to evaporate some of the water, leaving the essence of the dish in the finished sauce.

❋ Remember the 30-minute rule: If your dish will simmer more than 30 minutes, use a dried herb or spice; fresh herbs will lose their flavor in 30 minutes. At the end of the cooking time, add fresh herbs to refresh the flavor of the dish. The exceptions to this rule are fresh rosemary and fresh thyme sprigs, which are woody and can stand up to a long simmer.

❋ Keep a lid on it! Every time you lift the lid of your slow cooker, you lose 20 minutes of cooking time. I've factored two lifts into the cooking time for each recipe. If you have a stainless-steel cover, you won't be able to see what's going on, and curiosity is a natural instinct in a cook. Or you may want to turn the ingredients.

❋ Never fill your slow cooker more than two-thirds full; many cookers have a maximum fill line, but you can figure this out by looking at the insert. On the other hand, always fill the cooker at least halfway so your ingredients don't burn.

❋ Sauté meats, poultry, and aromatics such as garlic, onion, dried herbs, and spices before adding them to the slow cooker. Sautéing allows them to release some oil and bloom. If you just toss raw garlic and onion into the cooker, they will taste raw in the final dish.

❋ Meats and poultry should be sautéed so that the caramelized bits on the bottom of the skillet can be added to the slow cooker to enhance the flavor of the sauce. Raw meats tend to foam when simmering, and the foam is not only unsightly in the finished dish but also unappetizing.

❋ Never put frozen food into a slow cooker, which could cause your dish to breed bacteria. If you think about it, your food would have to defrost, then get back to a safe temperature, and cook to doneness.

It's a risk I won't take, although there are lots of books that recommend that you put frozen meats into the slow cooker.

❋ To prevent food from sticking to the cooker, use a slow-cooker liner, which is available in supermarkets and gourmet stores. Some dishes, such as casseroles, have a tendency to stick to the inside of your insert, making it difficult to clean. If you prefer, you can use a nonstick cooking spray. Either one will make cleanup simpler, which is why they're essential in my kitchen.

❋ Some slow cookers may cook hotter than others, so keep extra broth or liquid on hand in case the liquid in the cooker evaporates too quickly.

❋ Make sure you read your slow cooker manufacturer's instructions for operation and cleaning.

❋ When shopping for a slow cooker, look for a good-quality cooker, which should give you even heating. You do get what you pay for with electric cooking utensils. If you bought a slow cooker at your local discount store, chances are it will cook at the same temperature on low as it does on high. I recommend that people use inexpensive cookers *only* on low because they tend to cook at hot temperatures, and I have had dishes burn in them. My preference is to get a programmable slow cooker that will switch from high to low or low to warm after a designated period of time has elapsed. Three of the high-end manufacturers now offer slow cookers with an insert that can be used on the stove top, eliminating the need for a large skillet. After you sauté your flavor base ingredients or meat in the insert, you place it in the slow cooker, and you are good to go.

CONVERTING A FAVORITE RECIPE FOR A SLOW COOKER

If you would like to convert a recipe you make on the stove top or in the oven for your slow cooker, follow the suggested times below and use only half the amount of liquid in the recipe.

CONVENTIONAL OVEN OR STOVE TOP	SLOW COOKER
30 minutes	1½ hours high/3 hours low
1 hour	3½ hours high/6 to 7 hours low
2 hours	4½ hours high/9 to 10 hours low
3 hours	5½ hours high/10 to 11 hours low

A Mediterranean Pantry

Chances are if you are reading this book, you already have some Mediterranean ingredients in your pantry. Following is an annotated list of ingredients with suggestions for what to buy, which I hope will help you produce the best possible food in your slow cooker.

ANCHOVIES / Salty, tiny fish with a strong flavor, anchovies come canned in oil. Buy small tins of imported Spanish or Italian anchovies and drain off the oil before using.

BLACK PEPPER / Grind your pepper in a pepper mill, or grinder; the fresh taste is essential for this type of cooking. I own a set of gravity-operated pepper mills that will grind either salt or pepper when I turn them over. They make it so much easier, especially when you have sticky hands in the kitchen!

BROTHS AND HOMEMADE STOCKS / Many dishes will call for broth or stock, and you can use your favorite brand of broth or your own homemade stock. There are many choices, so pick what appeals to your taste. Some dishes call for a soup base or a demi-glace for a punch of flavor. I like to use Superior Touch Better Than Bouillon soup base, which comes in a variety of flavors; More Than Gourmet demi-glace; and Provimi demi-glace, which comes frozen.

CANNED TOMATOES / I prefer the San Marzano imported Italian tomatoes. They have a consistently good flavor, and I never seem to get just the stem ends, which happens frequently with American brands. Experiment to find a tomato brand that you like. Each growing season is different, and some years, one brand will be better than the others. If you are growing fresh tomatoes in your garden, plant a plum tomato plant. When harvesting, cut the tomatoes in half and freeze them. Peel and seed them to add to sauces and slow-cooker dishes (frozen tomatoes are easier to peel than fresh).

CAPERS / These small buds grow on a bush that is native to the Mediterranean. Capers are cured in either salt or brine. The brined version will do just fine, and you can find them in any supermarket; just drain off the brine. Capers add a piquant flavor to dishes, and are used extensively in many Mediterranean countries. The buds come in a tiny and a larger size; the larger capers will need to be chopped for most dishes.

CHEESE / Great cheeses abound in the Mediterranean, from Greek feta to Spanish Manchego, which are both made primarily from sheep's milk. Great cheeses can add flavor, texture, and even spice to a dish. Search out a cheese shop in your area; cheesemongers are usually knowledgeable and often they will order what you would like. The cheese person at the supermarket may also be the kid who unloads the milk truck, so chances are his knowledge isn't going to help on the night you are looking for a nice pecorino romano!

CURED AND SMOKED MEATS AND SAUSAGES / Where to begin? Many Mediterranean countries produce sausages, hams, and other cured and smoked meats prized for their exceptional flavor. In Italy there is prosciutto from Parma, salt-cured according to traditional methods, along with other *salumi*, and in Spain, Serrano ham and chorizo sausage. Portugal is known for its linguiça sausage; France, for its charcuterie, such as pâté; and Morocco, for its Merguez sausage. All are available in the United States, where some artisans make them according to old-world methods. Where possible, I have suggested alternatives for some hard-to-find items.

DRIED BEANS AND LENTILS / The packaged dried beans and lentils at the supermarket may be old, so I recommend that you buy them at a health or natural foods store from bins, where you can get exactly as much as you need. The

turnover at natural foods stores is usually rapid, which means you can depend on the beans being fresher. Old beans take forever to cook, so check the expiration date if you have packaged beans.

DRIED FRUITS / The dried fruits of the region—apricots, figs, dates, raisins, apples, and pears—all contribute to Mediterranean cuisine. I usually buy my dried fruits from bins at a local natural foods store, where I know the food turns over frequently and I will be getting plump fruits.

DRIED HERBS / Buy quality here; it will enhance your dishes. Always sauté dried herbs before adding them to the slow cooker; they need to develop their flavor before liquid is added. Avoid dried herbs that have been rubbed, like sage. When the herb is rubbed, it loses most of its essential oils. To make sure your dried herbs are fresh, give them the sniff test. If there is no aroma, it needs to be tossed, and a new one purchased. I usually buy my herbs and spices from Penzeys, a terrific source for hard-to-find herbs and spices (see Resources, page 184).

EXTRA-VIRGIN OLIVE OIL / Here you will get what you pay for. That inexpensive bottle on the shelf in the supermarket will probably be a blend of many different oils from around the Mediterranean, which the producers bought up after the premium olive oil had been pressed and bottled. Whatever you choose, buy a small bottle and taste it when you get it home. Olive oil, like salt, and wine, is a personal preference; some people like a peppery aftertaste, while others like a buttery flavor.

FRESH FRUITS AND VEGETABLES / Full-service supermarkets are getting the message that their customers are looking for locally grown and organic foods, and many markets have a special section for that produce. I shop farmers' markets; there is a terrific one here in San Diego, where I can get local fruits and veggies for less than those in the supermarket. I recommend that you buy organic and locally grown whenever possible. The finished dishes will be so much more delicious and authentic than if you use conventional produce that has been on planes, trains, and trucks to get to your local supermarket, having been picked a week or two before you buy it.

GARLIC / Heads of fresh garlic won't break the bank, and they are definitely tastier than any peeled or already minced preparation in your store. Elephant garlic is not the same, so steer clear. Look for closed heads that don't have any green sprouts starting, a sign the garlic is old and will not add much flavor, but may be bitter.

LEEKS / Leeks are part of the onion family, but are more closely related to green onions and spring onions, with a mild flavor and gorgeously green-tinted leaves. Leeks are grown in sand, so it is necessary to clean them thoroughly before cooking. The best way is to slice them in half lengthwise, and spread the layers apart to expose any sand or grit that may be hiding in the crevices.

OLIVES / Many full-service supermarkets have olive bars, and you can buy just the amount you need. Oil-cured olives have a unique flavor, quite different from brine-cured olives. So if a recipe calls for oil-cured olives, they are worth searching out.

ONIONS / Sweet yellow onions, which are at least 6 percent sugar, are my first choice in many cooking preparations. Vidalia, Walla Walla, Maui, Mayan Sweets, and Texas 1015 are all available in supermarkets. Common yellow onions are called for when the sweetness of a dish requires their stronger flavor for balance. Red onions can be substituted for either type of onion in recipes, adding color and depth of flavor. White onions are generally preferred raw as a garnish on many dishes. Shallots, another member of the onion family, have a bit of a garlicky flavor, and pack a lot of punch in a small package. Look for onions and shallots that aren't bruised, and are firm to the touch. The skin should be tight, and there shouldn't be any green sprouts at the top, which means they are old and will be bitter.

PAPRIKA / Not just for dusting on potato salads or deviled eggs, paprika actually has a flavor and an aroma. Smoked paprika is used in Spanish dishes, hot paprika kicks up the flavors in spicy foods, and sweet paprika is used extensively in North African dishes.

RED PEPPER FLAKES / Red pepper flakes are essential for many dishes in this book, lending a spicy, warm flavor to the finished dish. Red spices tend to go bad and lose their flavor fairly quickly, so if you still have the bottle of red pepper flakes that came with your spice rack, you will need to get rid of it and buy fresh. If the red pepper is brown in color, get rid of it. Always sauté red pepper flakes, as well as cayenne pepper, before adding any liquid to the pan, so they will bloom in the oil, giving you a balanced flavor and taking away any harsh taste.

SAFFRON / The dried stamens of the crocus plant, this herb adds an exotic flavor to risotto, paella, and many North African dishes. Although it is expensive, you will not need much to make a statement in your dishes.

SALT / I prefer to cook with sea salt—either coarse, which I grind, or fine, which I use straight out of the container. I also use fleur de sel, which is a finishing sea salt (to be sprinkled over a finished dish), and sometimes a flaky sea salt from Cyprus. I like Maldon salt for its clean, fresh taste, and I sprinkle it on dishes to flavor them while they cook, or sprinkle it on freshly cooked vegetables as they come off the heat. I am not fond of kosher salt. It has a processed aftertaste to my palate, but if it is your preference, then by all means, use it.

VINEGAR / You will need a good white wine vinegar, red wine vinegar, and balsamic vinegar for your Mediterranean dishes. Be sure to check labels; many red wine vinegars are a blend of distilled white vinegar and some red wine vinegar added for color. Check the type of wine that was used, too. A Chianti, Cabernet, Burgundy, or Zinfandel wine vinegar will last a long time in a cool, dry pantry, and serve you well.

White wine vinegars may also be blended, so check the label and buy one made with a single varietal, such as Chardonnay or Sauvignon Blanc.

A good balsamic vinegar from Modena, where it is traditionally made, is thick, syrupy, and sweet enough to serve over ice cream or strawberries. Supermarket balsamics tend to be red wine vinegar with sugar and caramel coloring, so be forewarned. You should expect to pay about $30/£10 for a bottle of balsamic that has been aged. Traditionally made, imported Italian balsamic vinegar aged for ten or twenty-five years is an expensive proposition, but you can find good-quality balsamic vinegars in gourmet markets and specialty retail stores.

That old commercial for canned soup comes to mind when I think of a steaming slow cooker filled with hearty soup; it's mmmmm good. Soup in the Mediterranean kitchen is simmered for long periods on the back of the stove as the cook goes about her other housework. Long-simmering soups filled with vegetables, bits of meat or poultry, beans, and maybe pasta or rice bubble away on stoves in every region of the Mediterranean. You can make these delicious, comforting soups, from Italian Minestrone (page 23) to Greek Egg and Lemon Soup (page 28), with just a bit of prep and then a long, low simmer.

Soups benefit from long simmering, and improve in flavor with 10 hours of cooking time. Leftovers usually freeze well, but you can also keep them in the refrigerator for a few days. When making soup, be sure to cut each ingredient so that it is bite-size. That way your family won't have to cut the vegetables or protein in the bowl.

Minestrone

A recipe from Italy's *cucina povera* ("cuisine of the poor"), minestrone is the original stone soup, meaning the ingredients are subject to the cook's whim, and just about anything can go into the pot. Its preparation begins with a flavor layer called a *battuto*, a mélange of onion, carrot, celery, herbs, tomato, and sometimes garlic. When the elements of the *battuto* are sautéed together, they form the flavor base. *Minestrone* literally means "without stock," and in days gone by, the vegetables provided the flavor for the soup broth. I think chicken or vegetable broth adds character and flavor to the soup, and I use either one when preparing it. The cut-up rinds from aged Parmigiano-Reggiano cheese add just the right amount of salt and still more flavor, making this soup a home run after a long day at the office.

In a large skillet, heat the olive oil over medium-high heat and sauté the onion, carrots, celery, and sage for 3 minutes, or until the onion begins to soften. Add the wine and tomatoes, and cook for another 3 to 4 minutes, to evaporate some of the liquid. Transfer the mixture to the insert of a 4- to 6-qt/3.5- to 5.5-L slow cooker, and stir in the broth and zucchini, green beans, lentils, escarole, cauliflower, and Parmigiano rind. Cover the cooker and cook for 4 to 5 hours on high, or 8 to 9 hours on low.

At the end of the cooking time, stir in the cooked pasta, season with salt and pepper if necessary, bring to serving temperature, and ladle into bowls. The soup will keep on the warm setting for up to 10 hours. Any leftovers will keep in the refrigerator for up to 4 days. Or freeze the soup without the pasta for up to 2 months.

SLOW COOKER SAVVY

Precooking the pasta will ensure that it won't absorb all the broth from the soup. I generally cook 1 lb/455 g of pasta, and freeze it in small portions for use in soups.

This soup makes a great vehicle for recycling leftover fresh vegetables and any cooked meat or poultry that you might have from another meal. Add the cut-up meat to the soup when you add the vegetables.

Ingredients

2 tbsp extra-virgin olive oil

1 large onion, finely chopped

4 medium carrots, coarsely chopped

4 ribs celery, coarsely chopped

1 tsp dried sage, rosemary, thyme, or oregano

½ cup/120 ml dry white wine, such as Pinot Grigio or Sauvignon Blanc, or dry vermouth

One 14½- to 15-oz/415- to 430-g can chopped tomatoes, with their juice

8 cups/2 L chicken or vegetable broth

2 medium zucchini, halved lengthwise and cut into ½-in/12-mm pieces

¼ lb/115 g green beans, ends trimmed, and cut into 1-in/2.5-cm pieces

1 cup/200 g brown lentils, rinsed and picked over for stones

1 large head escarole (preferable), Swiss chard, spinach, or kale, cut into 1-in/2.5-cm pieces

1 small head cauliflower, cut into florets

Two 3-in/7.5-cm chunks of rind from Parmigiano-Reggiano cheese, cut into small pieces

2 cups/230 g small pasta, such as ditali, tubetini, or even elbows, cooked al dente

Salt (*optional*)

Freshly ground black pepper (*optional*)

2 cups/455 g dried chickpeas, soaked overnight in water to cover

¼ cup/60 ml extra-virgin olive oil

1 large onion, finely chopped

3 ribs celery, coarsely chopped

3 medium carrots, coarsely chopped

One 14½- to 15-oz/415- to 430-g can chopped tomatoes, with their juice

6 cups/1.4 L chicken broth

Salt

Freshly ground black pepper

Couscous (page 142), for serving

Harissa (optional), for garnish

Moroccan Chickpea Broth for Couscous

La Table de Fès in Paris is a tiny restaurant serving some of the best Moroccan food I've had outside of Marrakech. Madame directs the dining room, while from the kitchen Monsieur serves up heaping bowls of couscous and this savory soup ladled on top before the main courses arrive. My son-in-law Eric's goal is to speak French so he can tell Madame how much he loves to eat there! This is a terrific warm-up on a cold night, filling your tummy with Moroccan goodness. I prefer to serve this with traditional couscous rather than Israeli, which is delicious in its own right, but not authentic for this dish.

Rinse the soaked beans and transfer to the insert of a 4- to 6-qt/3.5- to 5.5-L slow cooker.

Heat the olive oil in a large skillet over medium-high heat, and sauté the onion, celery, and carrots for 3 minutes, or until the onion begins to soften. Add the tomatoes, and transfer the mixture to the insert of the slow cooker. Stir in the broth, cover, and cook on high for 4 hours, or on low for 8 hours. At the end of the cooking time, season the soup with salt and pepper.

To serve the soup, spoon some of the couscous into a soup bowl, and ladle the soup generously over the couscous. Garnish with harissa, if desired.

SLOW COOKER SAVVY

Harissa is a North African hot sauce, which is the pride of Moroccan households. Each harissa is a bit different. At La Table de Fès, Madame places a bit in the ladle, then scoops up some of the soup, so the heat will spread throughout your bowl. Be forewarned, a little harissa goes a long way. You can find it at Middle Eastern grocers, full-service grocers, or gourmet retailers.

Spanish Meatball Soup

SERVES 8   MAKES ABOUT TWENTY
1-IN / 2.5-CM MEATBALLS

The region of Andalusia (Andalucía in Spanish) borders the Mediterranean along the southern Spanish coast. Spain was conquered at different periods in its history by the Greeks, Carthaginians, Romans, Goths, and Moors, and the foods of the region still retain influences from each of these invading armies. The meatballs, which are called *albóndigas* in Spanish, are often served in a saffron-flavored tomato sauce at tapas bars in Spain. They are made with veal and pork, also flavored with saffron, and in this soup they float in a rich chicken broth. I like to add greens like escarole to the soup to give it more body and flavor. Traditionally the meatballs are deep-fried and then added to the soup, but I have found that panfrying works as well. The meatballs can be made ahead of time and refrigerated or frozen before using in the soup.

TO MAKE THE SOUP / Heat the olive oil in a large skillet over medium-high heat. Add the onion and garlic and sauté for 3 minutes, or until the onion is softened. Add the tomatoes, and stir to combine. Transfer the mixture to the insert of a 5- to 7-qt/4.5- to 6.5-L slow cooker. Stir in the escarole, beans, and broth. Cover and cook on high while making the meatballs.

TO MAKE THE MEATBALLS / Put the saffron and bread in a large mixing bowl. Pour in the milk and let the bread soak for about 5 minutes, until it is softened. Add the veal, pork, garlic, parsley, salt, and pepper, stirring to combine the mixture. Using a portion scoop, form the meat into 1-in/2.5-cm balls. Heat the olive oil in a large skillet over medium-high heat, and brown the meatballs all over (they will not be cooked through).

Add the meatballs to the soup in the slow cooker and cook on high for 3 hours, or on low for 5 to 6 hours. The meatballs will be tender. Season the soup with salt and pepper, if needed, before serving.

SLOW COOKER SAVVY

When you purchase a bunch of flat-leaf parsley in the store, wash it and spin it dry in a salad spinner. Chop it in the food processor or by hand, and transfer it to a zipper-top plastic bag, with a paper towel inside to absorb moisture. Seal the bag and store in the freezer. You can use the parsley directly from the bag; it will not turn color as some other herbs do when you freeze them.

FOR THE SOUP

2 tbsp extra-virgin olive oil

1 large onion, finely chopped

1 garlic clove, minced

One 14½- to 15-oz/415- to 430-g can crushed tomatoes, with their juice

1 large head escarole, tough stalks removed, and cut into 1-in/2.5-cm pieces

Two 14½- to 15-oz/415- to 430-g cans small white beans, rinsed and drained

8 cups/2 L chicken broth

FOR THE MEATBALLS

1 tsp saffron threads, crushed in the palm of your hand

1 cup/55 g torn sturdy bread, such as a baguette or French loaf

¼ cup/60 ml milk

1½ lb/680 g ground veal

½ lb/225 g ground pork

2 garlic cloves, minced

¼ cup/15 g finely chopped fresh flat-leaf parsley (see Slow Cooker Savvy)

1½ tsp salt

½ tsp freshly ground black pepper

1½ cups/360 ml extra-virgin olive oil

Salt

Freshly ground black pepper

Tunisian Lentil and Lamb Soup

2 tbsp extra-virgin olive oil

2 lb/910 g lamb shoulder, excess fat trimmed, and cut into 1-in/2.5-cm pieces

Salt

1 large onion, finely chopped

2 garlic cloves, minced

½ tsp red pepper flakes

2 cups/400 g brown lentils, rinsed and picked over for stones

One 14½- to 15-oz/415- to 430-g can chopped tomatoes, with their juice

8 cups/2 L chicken broth

½ cup/30 g chopped fresh flat-leaf parsley

Freshly ground black pepper (optional)

Tunisia is bordered on the west by Algeria and on the east by Libya, and its cuisine is similar to that of its neighbors. Tunisians use lamb and lentils. The soup is delicious over rice or couscous, making it a hearty dish to serve on a cold winter's night.

In a large skillet, heat the olive oil over medium-high heat. Sprinkle the lamb with 1½ tsp salt. Brown the lamb, a few pieces at a time, transferring the browned meat to the insert of a 5- to 7-qt/4.5- to 6.5-L slow cooker. When all the lamb has been browned, add the onion, garlic, and red pepper flakes to the skillet, and cook for 3 minutes, until the onion begins to soften. Transfer the mixture to the slow cooker, and stir in the lentils, tomatoes, and broth. Cover and cook on high for 3 hours, or on low for 6 hours. The lamb will be tender.

Skim any excess fat from the surface of the soup and add the parsley. Taste for seasoning and add more salt and some black pepper, if you like, before serving.

Portuguese Kale and Sausage Soup

SERVES 6 TO 8

This traditional Portuguese soup, called *caldo verde*, is found in Portuguese enclaves here in San Diego and in Portuguese communities throughout the United States where their heritage and cuisine continue to be celebrated. The soup is spicy stick-to-your-ribs fare that will be welcomed by everyone in your household who comes in from the cold. Linguiça and chorizo sausage can be found in many supermarkets, but if you can't find either one, a garlicky smoked pork sausage will work.

In a large skillet, heat the olive oil over medium heat and cook the sausage, pricking the skin with the tip of a sharp knife to release some fat. When the sausage is browned, transfer it to the insert of a 5- to 7-qt/4.5- to 6.5-L slow cooker. Add the onion and garlic, and sauté for 3 minutes, or until the onion begins to soften. Add the kale to the skillet, and stir with the garlic, onion, and oil to coat. Transfer the contents of the skillet to the slow cooker insert, and stir in the broth and potatoes. Cover the slow cooker, and cook on high for 3 hours, or on low for 6 hours.

Skim the excess fat off the surface of the soup, season with salt and pepper, and serve.

2 tbsp extra-virgin olive oil

½ lb/225 g linguiça or Spanish (not Mexican) chorizo sausage

1 medium onion, finely chopped

1 garlic clove, minced

1½ lb/680 g kale, tough ends trimmed and thinly sliced

8 cups/2 L chicken broth

4 medium Yukon gold potatoes, scrubbed and cut into ½-in/12-mm pieces

Salt

Freshly ground black pepper

Greek Egg and Lemon Soup

2 tbsp extra-virgin olive oil

4 boneless, skinless chicken breast halves, cut into bite-size pieces

1 large onion, finely chopped

4 ribs celery, coarsely chopped

Zest of 1 lemon, cut into strips (see Slow Cooker Savvy)

4 baby artichokes

10 cups/2.4 L chicken broth

1 cup/115 g orzo

2 large eggs

Juice of 2 lemons (about ½ cup/120 ml)

Salt (optional)

Freshly ground black pepper (optional)

¼ cup/15 g finely chopped fresh flat-leaf parsley

The fragrance wafting from the slow cooker when you are simmering a Mediterranean soup is intoxicating, and this lemony recipe is no exception. Your family will want to peek under the lid to see what's going on under there. The chicken, artichoke, and broth mingle with orzo. A finish of egg mixed with lemon juice at the end of the cooking time knocks this one to the top of Olympus! There are as many versions of this soup, called *augolemono*, as there are cooks in Greece. This one was inspired by a friend who served it proudly as part of a multicourse Greek dinner.

In a large skillet, heat the olive oil over medium-high heat, and sauté the chicken until it turns white on all sides (it will not be cooked through). Transfer the chicken to the insert of a 5- to 7-qt/4.5- to 6.5-L slow cooker and set aside. In the same skillet, over medium-high heat, sauté the onion, celery, and lemon zest for 3 minutes, or until the onion begins to soften. Transfer to the insert.

Cut off the stem and the top ½ in/12 mm from each artichoke, and cut into quarters. Drop the quarters into the insert and pour in the broth. Cover and cook the soup for 2 hours on high, or 4 hours on low. Stir in the orzo, cover the cooker, and cook for another 1 to 1½ hours on high, or 2 hours on low. At the end of the cooking time, turn off the slow cooker and remove the insert from the heating element.

In a small mixing bowl, whisk together the eggs and lemon juice. Slowly pour 1 cup/240 ml of the hot soup into the egg and lemon mixture to temper it, and stir the egg and lemon mixture into the soup. Taste for seasoning and add salt and pepper if needed. Stir in the parsley and serve.

SLOW COOKER SAVVY

Store-bought lemons are usually coated with wax to preserve them during shipment. Before zesting, make sure you scrub the outside of your lemon with hot water and a plastic veggie brush to get off all the wax. Otherwise, the wax from the zest will float to the top of the sauce.

Nonna's Soup for the Soul

This is comfort food for me. Whenever I didn't feel well as a child, my *nonna* would make me this soup. For many years, I just called it Nonna's soup. It's basically chicken soup with escarole, kale, or chard, a few more veggies, and—the best part—eggs and nutty Parmigiano-Reggiano beaten together and added at the end. *Stracciatella*, the Italian name for the soup, means "torn apart," which is what the eggs and cheese look like when they hit the hot liquid in the cooker.

In a large skillet, heat the olive oil over medium-high heat, and sauté the onion, carrots, and escarole, turning in the oil to coat, until the onion begins to soften, about 3 minutes. Transfer the contents of the pan to the insert of a 5- to 7-qt/ 4.5- to 6.5-L slow cooker. Add the broth. Cover and cook on high for 3 hours, or on low for 5 to 6 hours. The escarole will be tender.

Remove the top from the slow cooker. In a medium mixing bowl, whisk together the eggs and ½ cup/60g of the cheese. Drizzle the egg mixture into the simmering soup, stirring as you are pouring it in. Season with salt and pepper if necessary, and serve the soup immediately, garnished with additional Parmigiano, if desired.

SLOW COOKER SAVVY

Feel free to add cut-up chicken or leftover cooked pasta to the soup, if desired.

2 tbsp extra-virgin olive oil

1 small onion, finely chopped

3 medium carrots, finely chopped

1 head escarole, kale, savoy cabbage, or Swiss chard, cored and cut into ½-in/12-mm pieces

8 cups/2 L chicken broth

4 large eggs

½ to ⅔ cup/60 to 75 g freshly grated Parmigiano-Reggiano cheese

Salt

Freshly ground black pepper (optional)

Vegetable Soup Provençal

2 tbsp extra-virgin olive oil,
plus ½ cup/120 ml

3 leeks (white and tender green parts),
halved lengthwise, cleaned, and cut crosswise into ½-in/12-mm half-moons

3 ribs celery, coarsely chopped

3 medium carrots, coarsely chopped

2 tsp herbes de Provence (see Slow
Cooker Savvy, page 114)

½ cup/120 ml dry white wine, such as
Pinot Grigio, Pinot Gris, or Sauvignon
Blanc, or dry vermouth

One 14½- to 15-oz/415- to 430-g can
chopped tomatoes, with their juice

8 cups/2 L chicken or vegetable broth

2 medium zucchini, ends trimmed,
and cut into ½-in/12-mm chunks

2 cups/340 g fresh shelled peas
or frozen peas, defrosted

1 head escarole, cut into 1-in/2.5-cm
pieces

Two 14½- to 15-oz/415- to 430-g cans
small white beans, rinsed and drained

2 cups/90 g firmly packed fresh
basil leaves

6 garlic cloves, peeled

Salt

Freshly ground black pepper

This colorful soup has the aroma of an herb garden when you lift the lid on the slow cooker. Filled with vegetables, it's the perfect soup to serve for lunch with a wedge of quiche or a *salade niçoise*. Natives of Provence add a pestolike garnish, which they call *pistou*. Fragrant with the scent of basil, it gives the soup a delicious flavor.

In a large skillet, heat the 2 tbsp olive oil over medium-high heat and sauté the leeks, celery, carrots, and herbes de Provence for 3 minutes, or until the carrots begin to soften. Add the wine, and cook to allow the wine to evaporate a bit. Transfer the contents of the skillet to the insert of a 5- to 7-qt/4.5- to 6.5-L slow cooker. Add the tomatoes, broth, zucchini, peas, escarole, and beans and stir to blend. Cover and cook on high for 2 hours, or on low for 4 hours.

In a blender or food processor, combine the basil and garlic and pulse on and off to break them up. With the machine running, add ¼ cup/60 ml of the olive oil. Scrape down the sides of the blender and taste. Add salt and pepper if necessary. If the pistou is very thick, add more olive oil, 1 to 2 tsp at a time. The pistou should hold together, and not be runny. Transfer the pistou to an airtight container, and float the remaining oil on the top to prevent the basil from discoloring.

When ready to serve, taste the soup for seasoning and correct by adding salt and pepper. Ladle the soup into bowls, and dollop 1 to 2 tbsp of pistou in the center of each serving.

Butternut Squash Soup with Crispy Prosciutto

In Italian this soup is called *la zuppa di zucca con prosciutto.* Loosely translated, *zucca* means "pumpkin," but Italian pumpkins are more like a butternut squash. Fortunately, butternut squash is readily available at your local market year-round. This smooth, creamy soup is scented with sage, flavored with apple, and topped with a crispy garnish of salty prosciutto, thus delivering creamy, crispy, sweet, and salty in one delicious serving!

Heat the olive oil in a large skillet over medium-high heat, and sauté the onion, apple, and sage for 3 minutes, or until the onion begins to soften. Transfer the mixture to the insert of a 5- to 7-qt/4.5- to 6.5-L slow cooker and stir in the squash and broth. Cover the slow cooker and cook on high for 3 hours, or on low for 6 hours.

When the soup is almost done, melt the butter in a small skillet over medium-high heat. Add the prosciutto and cook until crispy. Drain on paper towels.

Purée the soup right in the insert with an immersion blender, or cool the soup and purée in a blender or food processor. Add the cream, taste for seasoning, and add salt and pepper if needed. Serve the soup garnished with the crispy prosciutto.

2 tbsp extra-virgin olive oil

½ cup/80 g finely chopped onion

1 large Granny Smith apple, peeled, cored, and finely chopped

1 tsp dried sage (not rubbed)

One 3-lb/1.4-kg butternut squash, peeled and cut into 1-in/2.5-cm pieces (about 4 cups/910 g)

5 cups/1.2 L chicken or vegetable broth

2 tbsp unsalted butter

6 thin slices prosciutto, finely chopped

1 cup/240 ml heavy cream

Salt

Freshly ground black pepper (optional)

Creamy French Onion Soup

4 tbsp/55 g unsalted butter

1 tbsp extra-virgin olive oil

8 large sweet yellow onions, such as Vidalia, coarsely chopped

2 tsp dried thyme

1 tbsp sugar

1 cup/240 ml dry white wine, such as Pinot Grigio or Sauvignon Blanc, or dry vermouth

6 cups/1.4 L beef broth

2 tbsp beef soup base or demi-glace

Salt

Freshly ground black pepper

2 cups/230 g shredded Gruyère cheese

1 cup/115 g freshly grated Parmigiano-Reggiano cheese

8 slices French bread, toasted

A delicious combination of caramelized onions and beef broth, topped with a molten crown of melting cheese, French onion soup is my idea of the perfect weeknight dinner. If you like, serve it with a salad, quiche, or a sandwich. The soup is simple to put together; the long, slow simmer in the slow cooker gives a creamy texture to the onions, which practically melt into the broth. I recommend the addition of a beef soup base or demi-glace to the beef broth for an extra boost of beefy flavor. Your family will feel like they are dining in a lovely French bistro.

In a large skillet over medium-high heat, melt the butter with the olive oil and add the onions, thyme, and sugar, turning to coat the onions. Cook the onions until they begin to turn golden brown, 10 to 15 minutes. Add the wine, bring to a boil, and transfer the contents of the skillet to the insert of a 5- to 7-qt/4.5- to 6.5-L slow cooker. Add the broth and soup base. Cover and cook on high for 3 to 4 hours, or on low for 6 to 7 hours. Season with salt and pepper.

Preheat the broiler for 10 minutes. Saturate a dish towel with water and lay it on a baking sheet; the towel will help keep the soup bowls from sliding around. Combine the cheeses in a mixing bowl. Ladle the soup into ovenproof soup bowls or crocks. Float the toast on top of the soup, and sprinkle liberally with the cheese mixture. Arrange the bowls on the dish towel, and broil for 5 to 7 minutes, or until the cheese is golden brown.

Remove the bowls from the baking sheet and serve.

Slow Cooker Gazpacho

Gazpacho is typically served in Andalusia as a cold refresher, a sort of liquid salad, during the hot summer months. I turned the recipe on its head and created a hot soup with the same ingredients, topping it with a cold garnish. The garnish includes toasted bread crumbs, which give the soup a little added crunch and flavor.

TO MAKE THE SOUP / In a large skillet, heat the olive oil over medium-high heat and sauté the garlic, onion, and bell peppers for 3 minutes, until the onion begins to soften. Transfer the contents of the skillet to the insert of a 5- to 7-qt/4.5- to 6.5-L slow cooker. Stir in the broth, tomato purée, and vinegar. Cover and cook on high for 3 hours, or on low for 5 to 6 hours.

WHILE THE SOUP IS SIMMERING, MAKE THE GARNISH / In a mixing bowl, toss together the avocado, lemon juice and zest, cucumber, cherry tomatoes, and green onions.

Season the soup with salt and pepper, ladle into bowls, and dollop with the garnish. Sprinkle with bread crumbs and parsley before serving.

SLOW COOKER SAVVY

Cherry tomatoes are generally ripe no matter what time of year you buy them, unlike the lackluster winter plum tomatoes you will find in the supermarket, so they are my first choice for this garnish.

Slice French or Italian bread into ½-in/12-mm slices. Toast the bread in the oven or a toaster oven, until it is golden brown. Cool the bread, and crumble in a food processor, or place in a zipper-top plastic bag and crush with a meat tenderizer or rolling pin, until the bread has been reduced to crumbs.

FOR 1 CUP/115 G OR LESS: In a large nonstick skillet, over medium heat, add the bread crumbs, and toast, tossing occasionally until the crumbs begin to turn golden, this should take about 5 minutes. Remove the crumbs from the skillet immediately to stop the cooking process.

FOR MORE THAN 1 CUP/115G: Preheat the oven to 350°F/180°C/gas 4, and line a baking sheet with a silicone baking liner or parchment paper. Add the bread crumbs, and cook for 10 minutes, stirring once to turn the bread crumbs. Remove from the baking sheet immediately to stop the cooking process.

Bread crumbs will keep in an airtight container for up to 3 days, or frozen in zipper-top plastic bags for up to 1 month.

FOR THE SOUP

2 tbsp extra-virgin olive oil

3 garlic cloves, minced

1 large red onion, finely chopped

1 large yellow bell pepper, cored and finely chopped

1 large red bell pepper, cored and finely chopped

1 large green bell pepper, cored and finely chopped

4 cups/960 ml chicken or vegetable broth

One 28- to 32-oz/800- to 910-g can tomato purée

2 tbsp red wine vinegar

FOR THE GARNISH

2 Hass avocados, peeled, pitted, and finely diced

2 tsp fresh lemon juice

1 tsp grated lemon zest

1 English cucumber, finely diced

1 cup/230 g cherry tomatoes, quartered (see Slow Cooker Savvy)

2 green onions (white and green parts), finely chopped

Salt

Freshly ground black pepper

2 cups/230 g toasted bread crumbs (see Slow Cooker Savvy)

½ cup/30 g finely chopped fresh flat-leaf parsley

CH.02

MEATS
(PORK, LAMB, AND BEEF)

Pork, lamb, and beef are all found on the Mediterranean table. In many areas, goat is also a part of the diet. Since goat is not as widely available in the United States, it is not included here, but it can certainly be substituted in recipes calling for lamb. Pork is eaten smoked or cured, as well as freshly slaughtered. In the Mediterranean, all of the pig is used, including the blood for sausages.

Cheaper cuts of lamb, pork shoulder, and beef chuck become melt-in-your-mouth tender after a long simmer in the slow cooker. The resulting sauces are filled with the essence of the meat. Many cheaper cuts will sweat large amounts of liquid, in some cases up to 4 cups/960 ml, so be careful when adding liquids to the pot; too much will water down the sauce.

Dishes with similar ingredients and preparations can be found throughout the Mediterranean, from French Meatballs Languedoc (page 74) to Turkish Beef and Veal Meatballs (page 71) to Italian Bolognese Sauce (page 75). The common thread is meat that is cooked low and slow to coax out its flavor, for a succulent and delicious entrée.

Pork Braised with Dried Fruits and Cipollini Onions

SERVES 8

These aren't your mom's tough and chewy pork chops. They're falling-apart delicious, with a sweet-and-savory sauce combining sweet cipollini onions with golden raisins and dried apricots, flavored with the spices of North Africa. The sauce is wonderful served over buttered noodles or couscous. These little piggies are comfort food taken to the next level, and your family will be hanging around the pot and tapping their toes, waiting for dinner to be ready!

Season the pork on both sides with salt and pepper. In a large skillet, heat the olive oil over high heat, add the pork, and brown each chop on both sides. Transfer the pork to the insert of a 5- to 7-qt/4.5- to 6.5-L slow cooker. In the same skillet over medium-high heat, sauté the onions with the saffron and ginger until the outsides of the onions begin to soften slightly. Pour the broth into the pan, and scrape up any browned bits on the bottom. Transfer the contents of the skillet to the slow-cooker insert, and add the raisins, apricots, tomatoes, and broth, stirring to combine. Cover and cook on high for 4 to 5 hours, or on low for 8 to 10 hours, until the pork is tender.

Transfer the pork chops to a serving platter, and cover with aluminum foil. Transfer the sauce to a medium saucepan, and skim off any excess fat. Bring the sauce to a boil, add the cornstarch mixture, and whisk until the sauce returns to a boil and is smooth and thickened. Remove from the heat. Serve the pork chops napped with some of the sauce, and garnished with chopped cilantro. Pass the remaining sauce on the side.

SLOW COOKER SAVVY

Small, slightly sweet cipollini are a cousin of the pearl onion. To peel, bring 3 cups/720 ml of water to a boil in a saucepan, drop in the onions, and turn off the heat. After 3 minutes, remove from the water and drain. When cool enough to handle, cut off the root end of each onion; the peel should slip right off.

---

8 bone-in 1-in-/2.5-cm-thick pork loin chops (½ lb/225 g each)

Salt

Freshly ground black pepper

2 tbsp extra-virgin olive oil

24 cipollini onions, peeled and halved (see Slow Cooker Savvy)

8 threads saffron, crushed in the palm of your hand

¼ tsp ground ginger

1 cup/240 ml chicken broth

1 cup/170 g golden raisins

½ cup/85 g dried apricots, coarsely chopped

One 14½- to 15-oz/415- to 430-g can chopped tomatoes, with their juice

1 cup/240 ml beef broth

2 tbsp cornstarch mixed with ¼ cup/60 ml water

¼ cup/15 g finely chopped fresh cilantro, for garnish

Pork Braised with Pomegranates

6 medium carrots, cut into 1-in/2.5-cm pieces

2 tbsp extra-virgin olive oil

1 tsp turmeric

½ tsp ground cinnamon

1½ tsp salt

1 tsp freshly ground black pepper

6 bone-in 1-in-/2.5-cm-thick pork loin chops (½ lb/225 g each)

3 tbsp unsalted butter

2 large sweet yellow onions, such as Vidalia, finely chopped

¼ cup/60 ml pomegranate molasses

2 cups/480 ml chicken broth

1 cup/115 g finely chopped walnuts

½ cup/30 g finely chopped fresh flat-leaf parsley

2 tbsp cornstarch mixed with ¼ cup/60 ml chicken broth or water

1 cup/80 g pomegranate arils, for garnish

Opening a pomegranate is like opening a surprise package—inside are tiny little arils, seedlike in appearance, covered by a red waxy membrane. A great balance of sweet and tart, pomegranates are now found in almost every market—in the form of juice; or arils, separated from the fruit and waiting to be eaten; or the whole fruit, ready to be peeled. Pomegranates were eaten as far back as the exodus of the Jews from Egypt, as documented in the Bible.

Pomegranate molasses is the juice of the pomegranate, cooked down into a sticky, piquant syrup. A staple in North Africa and the Middle East, it packs a lot of pomegranate punch in small amounts. In this recipe it gives pork chops a sweet and smoky quality, making this a perfect dish to serve with couscous and a vegetable salad for dinner. It's a riff on a traditional Persian entrée called *fesenjan*, which is made with chicken, rather than pork. I prefer the pork because it soaks up all the lovely sauce and is melt-in-your-mouth delicious after its long, slow simmer.

Arrange the carrots in the insert of a 5- to 7-qt/4.5- to 6.5-L slow cooker. In a small bowl, combine the olive oil, turmeric, cinnamon, salt, and pepper to form a paste. Rub the paste into the pork.

Heat a large skillet over medium-high heat, and brown the chops on each side. Transfer the pork to the slow-cooker insert when browned. Melt the butter in the skillet, and cook the onions for 3 minutes, or until they begin to soften. Add the pomegranate molasses and broth and stir up any browned bits on the bottom of the pan. Pour the mixture over the chops. Cover the slow cooker and cook for 3 hours on high, or 5 to 6 hours on low.

Stir in the walnuts and parsley, cover, and cook for another 30 minutes on high, or 1 hour on low. Carefully remove the pork chops and carrots from the slow cooker using a large spatula, and transfer to a serving platter. Cover with aluminum foil.

Transfer the sauce to a saucepan, and bring to a boil. Add the cornstarch mixture, and whisk until the sauce returns to a boil and is smooth and thickened. Remove from the heat. Pour some of the sauce over the pork chops and carrots, and pass the remaining sauce on the side. Garnish the chops with the pomegranate arils before serving.

Braised Pork in Balsamic Vinegar

Succulent chunks of pork, redolent of sage, simmer in balsamic vinegar until the pork is fork-tender. The flavorful sauce is *molto buono* served over polenta, pasta, or garlic mashed potatoes.

Sprinkle the pork with the salt, pepper, and sage. In a large skillet, heat the olive oil over medium-high heat, and brown the pork on all sides, a few pieces at a time, trying not to crowd the pan and transferring the browned meat to the insert of a 4- to 6-qt/3.5- to 5.5-L slow cooker as it's done. Put the onions in the pan, and sauté until they begin to soften, about 3 minutes. Pour the vinegar into the pan, and scrape up any browned bits on the bottom. Transfer the onion mixture to the slow-cooker insert, turning the pork in the onions. Cover the slow cooker, and cook on high for 3 hours, or on low for 6 hours, until the pork is tender.

Remove the pork from the slow cooker, and skim any excess fat from the top of the sauce. Season the sauce with more salt and pepper if necessary. Return the pork to the sauce and keep warm until ready to serve.

SLOW COOKER SAVVY

Traditionally made balsamic vinegar from Modena is expensive; thick, syrupy, and sweet, it is delicious paired with fruit, or served over vanilla ice cream. The vinegar is made from the Trebbiano grape, and the traditional methods used by the consortium in Modena to produce it make it very expensive for both the maker and the buyer. The vinegar is aged in progressively smaller wooden barrels of various types, such as cherry, chestnut, and ash, for between five and twenty-five years, or even more. Many producers in the Modena-Reggio area say that their generation makes *balsamico* for the next one. In the United States, much of the supermarket balsamic vinegar is actually red wine vinegar with caramel color and added sugar. Buy good-quality balsamic vinegar, imported from Italy, and make it the best you can afford.

3 lb/1.4 kg boneless country-style pork ribs or pork shoulder, excess fat trimmed, and cut into 1-in/2.5-cm chunks

1½ tsp salt

½ tsp freshly ground black pepper

2 tsp dried sage (not rubbed)

2 tbsp extra-virgin olive oil

2 large sweet onions, coarsely chopped

1 cup/240 ml good-quality balsamic vinegar (see Slow Cooker Savvy)

Tuscan Milk-Braised Pork

1½ cups/360 ml whole milk

2 cups/480 ml heavy cream

Peel of 1 lemon, cut into strips

Leaves of 1 large bunch fresh sage (about 20), thinly sliced

One 4-lb/1.8-kg pork loin roast, tied with butcher's twine or silicone bands

Salt

Freshly ground black pepper

½ cup/120 ml extra-virgin olive oil

1 large sweet yellow onion, such as Vidalia, finely chopped

3 medium carrots, coarsely chopped

3 ribs celery, including the leaves, coarsely chopped

½ cup/120 ml dry white wine, such as Pinot Grigio or Sauvignon Blanc, or dry vermouth

A classic from the region of Tuscany, this simple dish features melt-in-your-mouth tender pork and a luxurious sauce flavored with white wine, lemon zest, and sage. Using a combination of milk and cream prevents the milk from curdling, which sometimes happens in the long cooking process. If you have an older slow cooker that overheats, cook this on the low setting, and if the sauce curdles, use a blender to smooth it out. There are differing opinions about the herbs to use in this dish, but I find the sage gives it a nice mellow flavor that pairs well with the lemony sauce.

Pour the milk and cream into the insert of a 5- to 7-qt/4.5- to 6.5-L slow cooker. Stir in the lemon peel and half the sage. Cover the slow cooker, set it to high, and set aside.

Sprinkle the pork evenly with salt and pepper. In a large skillet, heat 2 tbsp of the olive oil over high heat and brown the pork on all sides, turning frequently. Transfer the pork to the slow cooker, lower the heat under the skillet to medium-high, and add another 2 tablespoons of olive oil, the onion, carrots, and celery. Sauté for 3 minutes, or until the onion begins to soften. Pour in the wine and allow it to boil for 1 minute, scraping up the browned bits on the bottom of the pan. Transfer the contents of the skillet to the insert, stirring to blend with the other ingredients. Cover and cook on high for 4 hours, or on low for 8 to 10 hours, until the pork is tender.

While the pork is cooking, heat the remaining ¼ cup/60 ml oil in a small skillet, and fry the remaining sage leaves until crisp. Drain on paper towels and set aside. When the pork is done, transfer to a cutting board and cover with aluminum foil. Strain the sauce into a saucepan, and bring to a boil. Boil the sauce for 3 to 5 minutes to reduce and concentrate the flavors. Remove the butcher's twine from the roast and slice. Serve the roast on a platter, napped with some of the sauce and topped with the fried sage leaves. Serve the warmed sauce along-side the roast.

Portuguese White Wine–Braised Pork Loin with Roasted Red Peppers

Colorful roasted red peppers and a white wine and garlic-scented broth flavor this tender pork dish. At the end of the cooking time the broth and peppers are puréed, resulting in a sauce similar to a romesco. It's terrific when served over pasta, rice, or potatoes. And the leftover pork makes delicious panini.

In a large skillet, heat the olive oil over medium-high heat and sauté the onion, garlic, and paprika for 3 minutes, or until the onion begins to soften. Transfer the mixture to the insert of a 5- to 7-qt/4.5- to 6.5-L slow cooker, and stir in the roasted peppers and cherry tomatoes.

Sprinkle the pork evenly with the salt and pepper, and in the same skillet, brown the pork on all sides. Transfer to the slow cooker. Add the wine and soup base to the skillet, scrape up any browned bits on the bottom of the pan, and pour over the pork. Cover and cook on low heat for 7 to 8 hours, until the pork is tender.

Using tongs, remove the pork from the cooker. Skim off the excess fat, and stir in the hazelnuts, bread crumbs, and parsley. Using an immersion blender, purée the sauce. After the pork has rested for 10 minutes, remove the butcher's twine, and slice the pork ½ in/12 mm thick. Serve the pork napped with the sauce, and pass the remaining sauce on the side. The pork and sauce are delicious hot, warm, or at room temperature.

❧ SLOW COOKER SAVVY ❧

To roast bell peppers, preheat the broiler for 10 minutes. Arrange the peppers on a baking sheet lined with parchment paper or aluminum foil. Broil on all sides until the skin is charred. Turn off the broiler, close the oven door, and allow the peppers to cool in the oven. When the peppers are cool enough to handle, slip off the skins, remove the core, and cut the peppers into strips. The cooled, skinned peppers can be refrigerated for up to 3 days.

---

2 tbsp extra-virgin olive oil

1 large sweet onion, such as Vidalia, thinly sliced

8 garlic cloves, minced

1 tsp sweet paprika

6 roasted red bell peppers, either home-made (see Slow Cooker Savvy) or jarred, cut into thin strips

2 cups/240 g cherry tomatoes, halved

One 3½- to 4-lb/1.6- to 1.8-kg pork loin, tied at 1-in/2.5-mm intervals with butcher's twine or silicone loops

1 tsp salt

½ tsp freshly ground black pepper

1½ cups/360 ml dry white wine, such as Pinot Grigio or Sauvignon Blanc, or dry vermouth

2 tbsp beef soup base or demi-glace

½ cup/55 g chopped toasted hazelnuts

½ cup/55 g toasted bread crumbs (see Slow Cooker Savvy, page 35)

½ cup/30 g packed fresh flat-leaf parsley

Stuffed Pork Loin with Prunes and Port Wine

1 cup/240 ml ruby port

24 dried plums (Slow Cooker Savvy)

One 4-lb/1.8-kg pork loin roast

Salt

Freshly ground black pepper

2 tbsp extra-virgin olive oil

1 cup/160 g finely chopped shallots

2 tsp dried thyme

½ cup/120 ml Dijon mustard

½ cup/100 g firmly packed light brown sugar

2 cups/480 ml beef broth

2 tbsp cornstarch mixed with ¼ cup/60 ml water

½ cup/30 g finely chopped fresh flat-leaf parsley

This elegant dish comes from the Dordogne region, in southwestern France. The prunes there are as big as your fist, juicy and sweet. They give this dish a sweet flavor, which counterbalances the strong notes of the port wine sauce. In the Dordogne, this dish is usually served with potatoes sautéed in duck fat, but oven-roasted potatoes with a bit of garlic and rosemary are a fine alternative.

In a mixing bowl, pour the port over the dried plums and set aside to soak while preparing the pork. On a cutting board, butterfly the pork: Lay the pork loin down with an end close to you. Using a boning knife or other thin, flexible knife, cut lengthwise through the center of the roast from one end to the other, leaving a ¾-in/2-cm hinge of uncut meat. Spread out the meat and sprinkle with salt and pepper. Drain the plums, saving the port. Arrange 8 to 10 plums over half of the roast, and fold the meat over the plums. Tie with butcher's twine or silicone bands at 1-in/2.5-cm intervals.

Heat the olive oil in a large skillet over high heat and brown the pork on all sides. Transfer the meat to the insert of a 5- to 7-qt/4.5- to 6.5-L slow cooker. Add the shallots and thyme to the skillet, and cook for 3 minutes, until the shallots begin to soften. Transfer to the insert, and stir in the mustard, sugar, reserved port, remaining plums, and broth. Cover and cook on high for 4 to 5 hours, or on low for 8 to 10 hours, until the meat is tender. It will literally fall apart.

Transfer the meat and plums to a cutting board, and cover with aluminum foil. Strain the contents of the slow cooker into a small saucepan and skim off any excess fat. Bring the sauce to a boil. Whisk in the cornstarch mixture, and continue whisking until the sauce returns to a boil and is smooth and thickened. Remove from the heat.

Stir in the parsley, and keep the sauce warm while you slice the meat. Cut off the butcher's twine, and slice the meat ½ to ¾ in/12 mm to 2 cm thick. Serve the meat napped with some of the sauce and surrounded by the loose plums.

SLOW COOKER SAVVY

The word *prune* has gotten a bad rap. Prune growers in the United States are now labeling their fruits as "dried plums" to help counteract all the bad press. If your family won't eat them, regardless of what they're called, figs will work well in this recipe, and so will dried apricots.

Pork Shoulder Stuffed with Fennel, Garlic, and Rosemary

I could write love sonnets to this dish, otherwise known as *porchetta*—a stuffed and rolled pork shoulder sold all over the countryside in Umbria and Tuscany. This is peasant food, real food without pretense. *Porchetta* is usually served in a sandwich from a food truck, where mama has been roasting the pork for hours. The sandwich drips with roasted pork juices, smells of garlic and *rosmarino*, and crunches with crackling skin. It's heavenly eaten by the roadside with an Italian beer. *Porchetta* is a great choice for serving to a large crowd along with grilled vegetables, roasted potatoes, and salad. The slow cooker is the perfect place to cook a *porchetta*; it emerges falling-apart tender, and perfumes the house with fennel, rosemary, and garlic.

One 5- to 6-lb/2.3- to 2.7-kg boneless pork shoulder

1 tbsp salt

2 tsp freshly ground black pepper

½ cup/120 ml extra-virgin olive oil

6 garlic cloves, minced

2 tbsp finely chopped fresh rosemary

2 tsp fennel seeds

2 large onions, finely chopped

1 fennel bulb, wispy fronds removed, finely chopped

2 cups/480 ml dry white wine, such as Pinot Grigio or Sauvignon Blanc, or dry vermouth

Lay the pork on a cutting board, fat-side down, and sprinkle with some of the salt and pepper. In a mixing bowl, stir together the remaining salt and pepper, olive oil, garlic, rosemary, and fennel seeds. Rub this mixture all over the pork. Roll up the pork from a short side, and tie it at 1-in/2.5-cm intervals with butcher's twine or silicone loops.

Spread out the onions and chopped fennel on the bottom of the insert for a 5- to 7-qt/4.5- to 6.5-L slow cooker, and pour in the wine. Lay the pork on top of the vegetables. Cover and cook on high for 5 to 6 hours, or on low for 10 to 12 hours. The pork will be very tender. Remove the meat from the slow cooker, cover with aluminum foil, and allow to rest for 20 minutes.

Strain the contents of the slow cooker into a saucepan and skim off any excess fat. Bring the sauce to a boil and continue boiling until reduced by half. Cut off the butcher's twine, and remove any excess fat. Slice the meat ½ in/12 mm thick, or pull apart with two forks. Serve piled on a platter with the sauce on the side.

Lamb-Stuffed Cabbage Rolls

1 head savoy cabbage, cored

1½ lb/680 g ground lamb

½ cup/80 g finely chopped red onion

2 garlic cloves, minced

½ tsp dried oregano

½ tsp dried marjoram

1½ tsp salt

½ tsp freshly ground black pepper

1 large egg, lightly beaten

1 large onion, coarsely chopped

2 cups/480 ml chicken broth

1½ cups/360 ml full-bodied red wine such as Merlot, Burgundy, or Chianti

½ cup/30 g finely chopped fresh flat-leaf parsley

2 tbsp unsalted butter, softened

2 tbsp all-purpose flour

There are many versions of stuffed cabbage rolls throughout the Mediterranean region. Dried fruits and couscous are tucked inside cabbage rolls in North Africa; while in France, myriad forcemeats, like pâté, are wrapped inside the leaves and steamed in broth. But these lamb-stuffed cabbage rolls from Greece really tickled my taste buds, and I think you will love serving them to your family. They are made with savoy cabbage, which is milder than green cabbage. Stuffed with a spicy lamb mixture, the cabbage rolls simmer in wine and broth. They're terrific served over orzo pasta.

Bring 4 qt/3.5 L of water to a boil in a large stockpot over high heat. Remove 8 leaves of cabbage from the head, keeping them intact. Blanch the cabbage, 2 leaves at a time, in the boiling water for 30 to 45 seconds, or until the cabbage is soft. Remove from the water, drain, and cool. Coarsely chop the remaining cabbage, and transfer it to the insert of a 5- to 7-qt/4.5- to 6.5-L slow cooker.

In a large mixing bowl, mix together the lamb, red onion, garlic, oregano, marjoram, salt, pepper, and egg with your hands or a wooden spoon until the mixture comes together. Form the meat into eight ovals, and lay each in the middle of a blanched cabbage leaf. Fold in the sides over the meat, then roll the stem end over the meat and continue rolling tightly to the end.

Transfer the rolls to the insert of the slow cooker, arranging them on the chopped cabbage. Sprinkle the onion over the cabbage rolls, and pour in the broth and wine. Cover and cook for 3 hours on high, or 5 to 6 hours on low. The meat should register 170°F/77°C on an instant-read meat thermometer.

Gently lift the rolls from the slow cooker using tongs, transfer to a serving platter, and cover with aluminum foil. Strain the liquid into a saucepan, bring to a boil, and continue boiling for 5 minutes, until reduced by a quarter. Stir in the parsley. In a small bowl, knead together the butter and the flour. Whisk in the butter mixture, 1 tsp at a time, and continue whisking until the sauce returns to a boil and is smooth and thickened to your liking. Serve the cabbage rolls in a pool of the warm sauce, with additional sauce on the side.

Green Bean and Lamb Stew Provençal

Beautifully colored, fragrant with herbes de Provence, and filled with potatoes, green beans, and tender wine-soaked chunks of lamb, this one-pot meal is sure to please everyone in your family.

In a shallow dish, combine the flour, 2 tsp salt, and 1 tsp pepper. Dredge the lamb in the flour mixture. In a large skillet, heat 2 tbsp of the olive oil over medium-high heat, and brown the lamb, a few pieces at a time, turning to brown the meat on all sides. Transfer the browned lamb to the insert of a 5- to 7-qt/4.5- to 6.5-L slow cooker. Heat the remaining 2 tbsp olive oil in the same skillet, over medium-high heat, and sauté the garlic, shallots, and herbes de Provence for 3 minutes, or until the shallots begin to soften. Add the wine and tomatoes and stir to combine.

Transfer the contents of the skillet to the slow cooker and add the demi-glace, stirring to combine. Arrange the potatoes and the green beans on top of the lamb. Cover and cook on high for 4 hours, or low for 7 to 8 hours, until the lamb is tender.

Skim off any excess fat from the surface of the sauce, and if needed, season the stew with salt and pepper before serving.

½ cup/65 g all-purpose flour

Salt

Freshly ground black pepper

2½ lb/1.2 kg lamb shoulder, excess fat trimmed, and cut into 1-in/2.5-cm chunks

4 tbsp/60 ml extra-virgin olive oil

4 garlic cloves, sliced

½ cup/80 g finely chopped shallots

2 tsp dried herbes de Provence

1 cup/240 ml full-bodied red wine, such as Burgundy

One 14½- to 15-oz/415- to 430-g can crushed tomatoes, with their juice

1½ cups/360 ml beef demi-glace or ¼ cup/60 ml beef soup base dissolved in 1½ cups/360 ml water

1 lb/455 g tiny Yukon gold or assorted fingerling potatoes, scrubbed

1 lb/455 g green beans, ends trimmed, and cut into 2-in/5-cm pieces

Shepherd-Style Lamb of Crete

Salt

Freshly ground black pepper

4 garlic cloves, minced

Grated zest of 1 lemon

¼ cup/60 ml extra-virgin olive oil

3 lb/1.4 kg lamb shoulder, excess fat trimmed, and cut into 1-in/2.5-cm pieces

1 cup/240 ml dry white wine, such as Pinot Grigio or Sauvignon Blanc, or dry vermouth

4 baby artichokes, stems trimmed, and quartered lengthwise

½ lb/225 g tiny yellow potatoes or fingerlings

¼ cup/15 g finely chopped fresh flat-leaf parsley

Crete is the largest of the Greek isles. Ruled by the Venetians from about 1200 to the late 1600s, it is primarily a farming community. The Cretan diet (which includes a lot of fresh vegetables and olive oil) has been studied by researchers because the inhabitants of Crete have the lowest mortality rate, as well as the lowest rates of heart disease and cancer, in the entire region. This recipe is one that might be served after the slaughter of a lamb, as a celebration, or at a large family meal.

In a large mixing bowl, combine 1½ tsp salt, ½ tsp pepper, the garlic, lemon zest, and olive oil. Add the lamb to the bowl, and toss to coat with the mixture.

Heat a large skillet over high heat, and brown the lamb, a few pieces at a time, on all sides. Transfer the browned lamb to the insert of a 5- to 7-qt/4.5- to 6.5-L slow cooker. Add the wine to the skillet and bring to a boil, scraping up the browned bits on the bottom of the pan. Pour the wine over the lamb in the slow cooker, and arrange the artichokes and potatoes in the insert. Cover and cook on high for 3 hours, or on low for 6 hours, until the lamb, artichokes, and potatoes are tender (the sharp tip of a paring knife should go into a vegetable without any resistance).

Transfer the lamb and vegetables to a serving platter, and cover with aluminum foil to keep warm. Skim any excess fat from the sauce, stir in the parsley, and season with salt and pepper. Pour the sauce over the lamb and vegetables and serve.

Syrian-Style Lamb with Saffron

This brilliantly colored braised lamb has an exotic quality about it from the addition of saffron and orange zest. Terrific to serve with Pilaf (page 141) or over potatoes or pasta, it makes a lovely party dish. And it goes together so easily in your slow cooker, which seems to melt the lamb into succulent bits. A swirl of yogurt at the end transforms the cooking liquid into a delicious sauce, which will guarantee your family's membership in the clean-plate club.

In a large skillet over medium-high heat, melt the butter with the olive oil. Sprinkle the meat evenly with 1½ tsp salt, and brown in batches, being careful not to crowd the pan. Transfer the browned meat to the insert of a 5- to 7-qt/4.5- to 6.5-L slow cooker. Add the onions, garlic, saffron, cinnamon, and cayenne to the pan, and sauté until the onions are translucent, 7 to 10 minutes. Add the chicken broth and bring to a boil, scraping up any browned bits on the bottom of the pan. Transfer the contents of the skillet to the slow cooker insert and add the beef broth, stirring to combine. Cover and cook on high for 4 hours, or on low for 7 to 8 hours, until the lamb is tender.

Skim off any excess fat from the surface of the stew, and stir in the orange zest and mint. Turn off the slow cooker and allow the dish to rest for 10 minutes. Stir in the yogurt, taste for seasoning, and add salt or pepper if necessary. Serve the stew over rice, pasta, or potatoes.

SLOW COOKER SAVVY

High heat will curdle yogurt, so it's best to let the sauce rest a few minutes before whisking in the yogurt.

2 tbsp unsalted butter

2 tbsp extra-virgin olive oil

2 lb/910 g lamb shoulder meat, excess fat trimmed, and cut into 1-in/2.5-cm cubes

Salt

2 large sweet yellow onions, such as Vidalia, thinly sliced

2 garlic cloves, sliced

1 tsp saffron, crushed in the palm of your hand

¼ tsp ground cinnamon

Pinch of cayenne pepper

1 cup/240 ml chicken broth

1½ cups/360 ml beef broth

Grated zest of 1 large navel orange

¼ cup/15 g finely chopped fresh mint

1 cup/240 ml Greek-style yogurt

Freshly ground black pepper (optional)

Cooked rice, pasta, or potatoes, for serving

Potato-Smothered Lamb from Calabria

¼ cup/60 ml extra-virgin olive oil

8 garlic cloves, minced

1 tbsp finely chopped fresh rosemary

1 cup/60 g finely chopped fresh flat-leaf parsley

½ cup/60 g freshly grated pecorino romano cheese

One 28- to 32-oz/800- to 910-g can plum tomatoes, drained and chopped

2 tsp salt

1 tsp freshly ground black pepper

1½ lb/680 g Yukon gold potatoes, thinly sliced

2½ lb/1.2 kg lamb shoulder or leg of lamb, excess fat trimmed, and cut into 1-in/2.5-cm pieces

1 cup/240 ml chicken broth

Food from the farm is some of the most delicious in the Mediterranean; the home cook improvises using ingredients on hand. This dish is from the hills of Calabria, a region of Italy at the toe of the boot that is relatively poor. Calabrian cooks make many one-pot meals. This one is a great example of how a few ingredients can meld together to make an incredibly tasty dish. The lamb, which cooks between layers of garlicky potatoes flavored with rosemary and tomatoes, turns meltingly tender. A simple salad dressed with olive oil and lemon juice makes this a meal fit for a king. If you like, you can substitute oregano or sage for the rosemary.

In a small bowl, combine the olive oil, garlic, rosemary, parsley, cheese, tomatoes, salt, and pepper. Line the insert of a 5- to 7-qt/4.5- to 6.5-L slow cooker with a slow-cooker liner, or coat the interior with nonstick cooking spray.

Cover the bottom of the slow cooker with a quarter of the tomato mixture. In layers add half of the potatoes, another quarter of the tomato mixture, and then all the lamb. Spread another quarter of the tomato mixture over the lamb, layer with the remaining potatoes, and end with the remaining tomato mixture. Pour the broth over the potatoes and lamb. Cover the slow cooker and cook on high for 4 hours, or on low for 8 to 10 hours, until the lamb is tender.

Serve the lamb from the slow cooker, making sure each diner gets some of the potatoes as well as the meat.

Braised Leg of Lamb with Garlic

The flavor of the dish will vary, depending on the herbs you choose. A Provençal lamb dish might be cooked with herbes de Provence, while an Italian lamb will be fragrant with rosemary or sage, a Greek lamb dish is likely to contain oregano and maybe lemon zest, and North African lamb is often perfumed with paprika, cumin, and a finish of mint. So take a cruise on the Mediterranean and choose your own flavor palate for this simple dish. Serve with roasted potatoes or Pilaf (page 141) and roasted vegetables.

In a small bowl, combine 2 tsp salt, 1 tsp pepper, the garlic, herbes de Provence, and 2 tbsp of the olive oil to form a paste. Open up the lamb, and rub with the mixture on the top and bottom of the meat. Roll up the lamb into a compact cylinder, and tie with butcher's twine or silicone bands at 1-in/2.5-cm intervals.

Heat the remaining 2 tbsp olive oil in a large skillet over high heat, and brown the lamb on all sides. Transfer the lamb to the insert of a 5- to 7-qt/4.5- to 6.5-L slow cooker. In the same skillet, sauté the onions for 3 minutes, or until they begin to soften. Add the wine to the pan, bring to a boil, and scrape up any browned bits on the bottom of the pan. Transfer the onion and wine mixture to the insert and stir in the broth. Cover and cook on low for 8 to 9 hours, until the meat is tender.

Using tongs, carefully remove the lamb from the insert, transfer to a cutting board, and cover with aluminum foil. Strain the cooking liquid into a saucepan and bring to a boil. In a small bowl, knead together the butter and flour. Whisk the butter mixture into the liquid, 1 tsp at a time, and continue whisking until the sauce returns to a boil and is smooth and thickened to your liking. Season with salt and pepper if needed, and whisk in the parsley. Remove the butcher's twine from the lamb, and carve into slices. Serve the lamb with the warm sauce on the side.

Salt

Freshly ground black pepper

6 garlic cloves, minced

2 tsp herbes de Provence (see Slow Cooker Savvy, page 114)

4 tbsp/60 ml extra-virgin olive oil

One 4-lb/1.8-kg boneless butterflied leg of lamb

2 large sweet yellow onions, such as Vidalia, coarsely chopped

1½ cups/360 ml full-bodied red wine, such as Burgundy, Merlot, or Zinfandel

2 cups/480 ml beef broth

2 tbsp unsalted butter, softened

2 tbsp all-purpose flour

¼ cup/15 g finely chopped fresh flat-leaf parsley

✦ VARIATION ✦

Italian Lamb
Substitute rosemary or sage for the herbes de Provence and add one 14½- to 15-oz/415- to 430-g can chopped tomatoes, drained, to the slow cooker along with the wine and onion mixture.

Greek Lamb
Substitute chopped fresh oregano for the herbes de Provence, and add the grated zest of 1 lemon to the wine and broth before covering the slow cooker.

North African Lamb
Substitute 1 tsp of sweet paprika and 1 tsp of ground cumin for the herbes de Provence, and substitute fresh mint for the chopped parsley.

Braised Lamb Shanks with Red Wine and Oregano

FOR THE MARINADE

1½ tsp salt

½ tsp freshly ground black pepper

One 750-ml bottle full-bodied red wine, such as Barolo, Barbera, Chianti, or Merlot

8 garlic cloves, minced

¼ cup/60 ml extra-virgin olive oil

2 tsp dried oregano

2 tbsp honey

6 meaty ¾- to 1-lb/340- to 455-g lamb shanks

2 tbsp extra-virgin olive oil

3 large sweet yellow onions, such as Vidalia, coarsely chopped

4 garlic cloves, minced

3 medium carrots, coarsely chopped

⅛ tsp red pepper flakes

1 tsp dried oregano

Two 28- to 32-oz/800- to 910-g cans chopped tomatoes, with their juice

Salt

Freshly ground black pepper (optional)

¼ cup/15 g finely chopped fresh flat-leaf parsley

Grated zest of 1 orange (about 2 tbsp)

Braised lamb shanks are both rustic and elegant at the same time. Bathed in a deeply flavored red wine and tomato sauce and then sprinkled with orange zest, the lamb is falling-apart tender. It's scrumptious served over polenta, risotto, or wide pasta like pappardelle. Plan ahead when making the shanks, as you will need to marinate them overnight before simmering them in the slow cooker. There is usually enough sauce left over to freeze for a pasta dinner.

TO MAKE THE MARINADE / In a large mixing bowl, whisk together the salt, pepper, red wine, garlic, olive oil, oregano, and honey.

Put the lamb in a large zipper-top plastic bag and pour in marinade. Seal the bag and refrigerate for at least 8 and up to 24 hours.

When ready to cook, remove the lamb shanks from the bag, and arrange in the insert of a 5- to 7-qt/4.5- to 6.5-L slow cooker. Reserve the marinade.

In a large skillet, heat the olive oil over medium-high heat. Sauté the onions, garlic, carrots, red pepper flakes, and oregano until the onion is softened, about 5 minutes. Add the reserved marinade, bring to a boil, and continue boiling for 3 minutes. Transfer the contents of the skillet to the insert, and stir in the tomatoes. Cover the slow cooker and cook on high for 5 hours, or on low for 8 to 10 hours, until the lamb is tender.

Carefully remove the lamb from the sauce; it will be falling off the bones, so use a set of tongs to keep the meat together. Cover the lamb with aluminum foil. Skim off any excess fat from the sauce, taste for seasoning, and add more salt and pepper if needed. Stir in the parsley and orange zest. Serve the lamb shanks dressed in the sauce.

Lamb Stuffed with Artichokes and Braised in Lemon and White Wine

This stunning dish is a Provençal treatment of a lamb loin, which is stuffed with artichokes and simmered in a lemon and white wine sauce. It's a perfect main course to serve in the spring over mashed potatoes flavored with Boursin cheese, accompanied by roasted baby rainbow carrots.

Lay a lamb loin on a cutting board, with an end facing you. Make a lengthwise cut through the center of the loin, cutting from one end to the other, and leaving a ¾-in/2-cm hinge of uncut meat. Open up the loin, and flatten using a meat tenderizer so that the loin is an even thickness, about ½ in/12 mm. Repeat with the second loin. Make a paste from the mustard, 2 garlic cloves, salt, and pepper and rub the loins with the mixture on top and underneath.

In a large skillet, heat 2 tbsp of the olive oil over medium-high heat. Sauté the remaining 4 garlic cloves, the artichoke hearts, 1 tsp of the tarragon, and the lemon zest until the liquid in the pan has evaporated. Sprinkle the mixture with 2 tbsp of the lemon juice and allow to cool. Spread the mixture evenly over the prepared lamb loins, fold the meat over the filling, and tie with butcher's twine or secure with silicone bands at 1-in/2.5-cm intervals.

Stir together the remaining 2 tbsp lemon juice, the remaining tarragon, wine and demi-glace. Pour into the insert of a 5- to 7-qt/4.5- to 6.5-L slow cooker. Heat the remaining olive oil in the same skillet over high heat, and brown the lamb on all sides. Transfer to the slow cooker. Cover and cook on high for 1 hour, or on low for 2 hours, or until the meat registers 140°F/60°C on an instant-read meat thermometer.

Using tongs, remove the lamb from the slow cooker and transfer to a cutting board. Cover with aluminum foil. Strain the cooking liquid into a small saucepan, and bring to a boil. In a small bowl, knead together the butter and the flour. Whisk in the butter mixture, 1 tsp at a time, and continue whisking until the sauce returns to a boil and is smooth and thickened to your liking. Cut the butcher's twine from the lamb. Slice the lamb 1 in/2.5 cm thick, nap with some of the warm sauce, and pass the rest of the sauce on the side when serving.

Two 2-lb/910-g lamb loins, trimmed of excess fat

¼ cup/60 ml Dijon mustard

6 garlic cloves, minced

1½ tsp salt

1 tsp freshly ground black pepper

3 tbsp extra-virgin olive oil

One 10-oz/280-g package frozen artichoke hearts, defrosted and coarsely chopped

2 tsp dried tarragon

Grated zest of 2 lemons

4 tbsp/60 ml fresh lemon juice

1 cup/240 ml dry white wine, such as Pinot Grigio or Sauvignon Blanc, or dry vermouth

¼ cup/60 ml veal demi-glace or chicken soup base

2 tbsp unsalted butter, softened

2 tbsp all-purpose flour

Old-Fashioned French Beef Stew

8 strips thick-cut bacon, cut into ½-in/12-mm pieces

3½ to 4 lb/1.6 to 1.8 kg beef chuck, excess fat trimmed, and cut into 1-in/2.5-cm chunks

1 tsp salt

½ tsp freshly ground black pepper

½ cup/80 g finely chopped shallots

3 medium carrots, finely chopped

2 tsp dried thyme

2 bay leaves

¼ cup/60 ml tomato paste

½ cup/120 ml full-bodied red wine, such as Burgundy, Merlot, or Barolo

2 cups/480 ml beef broth

2 tbsp unsalted butter, softened

2 tbsp all-purpose flour

½ cup/30 g finely chopped fresh flat-leaf parsley

A kissing cousin to beef in Burgundy wine, this comfort food for the Gallic soul soothes and warms the body on cold winter nights. Served in bistros all over France, it is flavored with tomato, a bit of red wine, thyme, and bay leaves. It's perfect served over buttered noodles or with creamy mashed potatoes.

In a large skillet, cook the bacon over medium-high heat until it is crisp, and transfer to the insert of a 5- to 7-qt/4.5- to 6.5-L slow cooker. Drain all but 2 tbsp of the bacon drippings from the pan. Sprinkle the beef with the salt and pepper and brown the meat, in batches if necessary, transferring the browned pieces to the slow-cooker insert. Add the shallots, carrots, thyme, and bay leaves to the skillet, and sauté until the shallots begin to soften, about 3 minutes. Add the tomato paste and wine and bring to a boil, scraping up any browned bits on the bottom of the pan. Transfer the mixture to the slow cooker insert, and stir in the broth. Cover and cook on high for 4 hours, or on low for 8 hours, until the beef is tender.

Carefully remove the meat from the sauce, using a slotted spoon, and transfer to a tureen or serving bowl. Pour the sauce into a saucepan, remove the bay leaves, and bring the sauce to a boil. Knead the butter and flour together in a small bowl. Whisk the butter mixture into the sauce, 1 tsp at a time, and continue whisking until the sauce returns to a boil and is smooth and thickened to your liking. Stir in the chopped parsley, and pour the sauce over the beef in the bowl. Serve immediately.

Moroccan-Style Beef

This savory stew is filled with chickpeas, carrots, and succulent chunks of beef, which are tinted red by the generous quantity of paprika. It's a great party dish to serve with couscous and a red onion and orange salad, dressed with red wine vinegar and olive oil.

In a mixing bowl, combine the olive oil, garlic, salt, saffron, cumin, and paprika to form a loose paste. Rub half of the mixture into the beef and set aside. Put the onions and carrots in the insert of a 5- to 7-qt/4.5- to 6.5-L slow cooker, and drizzle the remaining paste over the vegetables, tossing them to coat.

In a large skillet over high heat, brown the meat, a few pieces at a time, transferring the browned pieces to the slow-cooker insert. Pour the broth into the skillet and bring to a boil, scraping up any browned bits on the bottom of the pan. Pour the broth and chickpeas into the slow cooker and stir to blend the ingredients. Cover and cook on high for 4 to 5 hours, or on low for 8 to 10 hours, until the meat is tender.

Carefully transfer the meat and vegetables to a serving bowl using a slotted spoon. Pour the sauce into a saucepan, and bring to a boil. Taste the sauce for seasoning and add pepper if necessary. In a small bowl, knead together the butter and flour. Whisk the butter mixture into the sauce, 1 tsp at a time, and continue whisking until the sauce returns to a boil and is smooth and thickened to your liking. Pour the sauce over the meat and vegetables in the serving bowl. Garnish with cilantro and parsley and serve.

¼ cup/60 ml extra-virgin olive oil

5 garlic cloves, minced

2 tsp salt

1 tsp saffron, crushed in the palm of your hand

1 tsp ground cumin

1 tbsp sweet paprika

3 lb/1.4 kg beef chuck, excess fat trimmed, and cut into 1-in/2.5-cm pieces

2 large sweet yellow onions, such as Vidalia, coarsely chopped

4 medium carrots, cut into 1-in/2.5-cm chunks

2 cups/480 ml beef broth

Two 14½- to 15-oz/415- to 430-g cans chickpeas, drained and rinsed

Freshly ground black pepper (optional)

2 tbsp unsalted butter, softened

2 tbsp all-purpose flour

¼ cup/15 g finely chopped fresh cilantro, for garnish

¼ cup/15 g finely chopped fresh parsley, for garnish

Beef Bracciole

Thin slices of round steak are rolled around prosciutto and Fontina cheese and simmered in a red wine and tomato sauce flavored with rosemary. The result is a delicious stick-to-your-ribs entrée for winter dining, which you can serve over pasta, polenta, roasted potatoes, risotto, or farro. Or serve the bracciole at room temperature for a patio supper.

4 tbsp/60 ml extra-virgin olive oil

2 garlic cloves, minced

1 large onion, finely chopped

3 medium carrots, finely chopped

1 tbsp finely chopped fresh rosemary

1 cup/240 ml full-bodied red wine, such as Barolo, Chianti, Merlot, or Zinfandel

One 28- to 32-oz/800- to 910-g can chopped tomatoes, with their juice

2 lb/910 g round steak, sliced ¼ in/6 mm thick (see Slow Cooker Savvy)

Salt

Freshly ground black pepper

8 thin slices prosciutto (about ¼ lb/115 g total)

8 slices Italian Fontina cheese

½ cup/30 g finely chopped fresh flat-leaf parsley

In a large skillet, heat 2 tbsp of the olive oil over medium-high heat and sauté the garlic, onion, carrots, and rosemary for 3 minutes, until the onion begins to soften. Add the wine and bring to a boil, scraping up any browned bits on the bottom of the pan. Transfer the mixture to the insert of a 5- to 7-qt/4.5- to 6.5-L slow cooker, and stir in the tomatoes. Cover and set on high while preparing the meat.

Lay the steak on a cutting board and sprinkle with salt and pepper. Lay a piece of prosciutto and a slice of Fontina on each piece of meat. Roll the meat from the short end, tucking in the sides, to form a compact package and secure with a toothpick, butcher's twine, or silicone bands. Heat the remaining 2 tbsp oil in the same skillet, and brown the beef on all sides. Transfer the meat to the slow cooker. Cover and cook on high for 3 hours, or on low for 6 hours, until the beef is tender, and the filling registers 170°F/77°C on an instant-read thermometer.

Remove the meat from the sauce, and cover loosely with aluminum foil. Skim off any excess fat from the sauce, and stir in the parsley. Remove the toothpick from each beef roll. Slice the rolls into three or four pieces and arrange on dinner plates, or on a serving platter. To serve, spoon some of the warm sauce over the rolls, and pass the remaining sauce on the side.

SLOW COOKER SAVVY

Top round is generally a smaller piece of meat than bottom round, and it will be a bit more tender, with some marbling. Your butcher can slice the meat into ¼-in/6-mm slices for you. Many supermarkets sell this cut as "minute steaks." Should you purchase bottom round, cut each slice into three pieces, and then roll up as directed.

Beef Pizzaiola

Beef bathed in an oregano-scented tomato sauce makes a terrific weeknight dinner when paired with pasta or polenta. A sprinkling of freshly grated Parmigiano-Reggiano over each serving completes the picture.

TO MAKE THE SAUCE / In a large skillet, heat the olive oil over medium-high heat and add the garlic, onion, and oregano. Sauté for 3 minutes, or until the onion begins to soften. Add the wine and bring to a boil. Transfer the mixture to the insert of a 5- to 7-qt/4.5- to 6.5-L slow cooker. Stir in the tomatoes. Cover the slow cooker and cook on low while preparing the meat.

TO MAKE THE MEAT / Sprinkle the beef with the salt and pepper. Heat the olive oil in a large skillet over medium-high heat, and brown the meat, a few pieces at a time. Transfer the browned meat to the slow cooker. Cover and cook on high for 4 hours, or on low for 6 to 7 hours, until the beef is tender.

Skim any excess fat from the sauce, taste for seasoning, and stir in the parsley. Serve the meat and sauce over pasta or polenta, sprinkled with Parmigiano-Reggiano.

FOR THE PIZZAIOLA SAUCE

2 tbsp extra-virgin olive oil

3 garlic cloves, minced

1 large onion, finely chopped

2 tsp dried Greek or Italian oregano

1 cup/240 ml full-bodied red wine, such as Burgundy, Merlot, or Barolo

Two 28- to 32-oz/800- to 910-g cans chopped tomatoes, with their juice

FOR THE MEAT

3 lb/1.4 kg beef sirloin, cut into 1-in/2.5-cm chunks

1½ tsp salt

½ tsp freshly ground black pepper

¼ cup/60 ml extra-virgin olive oil

¼ cup/15 g finely chopped fresh flat-leaf parsley

Cooked penne or farfalle pasta or polenta, for serving

Freshly grated Parmigiano-Reggiano cheese, for serving

Beef in Barolo

One 750-ml bottle Barolo

4 garlic cloves, minced

1 tbsp finely chopped fresh rosemary

1 tsp dried sage (not rubbed)

2 bay leaves

Salt

Freshly ground black pepper

4 tbsp/60 ml extra-virgin olive oil

One 4-lb/1.8-kg boneless chuck roast (see Slow Cooker Savvy), trimmed of excess fat

¼ lb/115 g pancetta, finely chopped

2 large yellow onions, finely chopped

4 medium carrots, finely chopped

3 ribs celery, including some of the leaves, finely chopped

2 oz/55 g dried porcini mushrooms, crumbled

3 tbsp soup base or demi-glace

2 tbsp unsalted butter, softened

2 tbsp all-purpose flour

¼ cup/15 g finely chopped fresh flat-leaf parsley

Barolo has been called the king of Italian wines, with a tradition that goes back to the mid-nineteenth century. Grown in the Piedmont region in Northern Italy, Barolo is a wine that should be served with strong flavors, rather than delicate ones. Beef in Barolo is the quintessential Italian pot roast. The beef marinates in the wine, which also permeates the liquid in the slow cooker. Traditionally served with risotto, this dish is equally delicious served over mashed potatoes Parmigiano or a wide, flat pasta, like pappardelle. I have even served beef in Barolo tucked into crusty rolls for Italian sliders! A heads-up: the beef marinates for 12 hours before it goes into the slow cooker.

In a mixing bowl, whisk together the wine, garlic, rosemary, sage, bay leaves, 2 tsp salt, 1 tsp pepper, and 2 tbsp of the olive oil. Place the roast in an extra-large zipper-top plastic bag, and pour the marinade over the beef. Seal the bag and refrigerate for at least 12 hours, and up to 24 hours. Remove the beef from the bag, saving the marinade, and pat dry.

In a large skillet, heat the remaining 2 tbsp olive oil over high heat, and brown the meat on all sides. Transfer the meat to the insert of a 5- to 7-qt/4.5- to 6.5-L slow cooker. Add the pancetta to the skillet, reduce the heat to medium-high, and cook until it renders some fat. Add the onions, carrots, celery, and porcini and sauté for 3 minutes, or until the onion begins to soften. Add the marinade to the skillet, stir in the soup base, and bring to a boil. Continue boiling for 3 minutes, scraping up any browned bits on the bottom of the pan. Transfer the contents of the skillet to the slow cooker insert. Cover and cook on low for 8 to 9 hours, until the meat is fork-tender.

Remove the meat from the insert, and cover with aluminum foil. Discard the bay leaves, transfer the contents of the insert to a large saucepan, and bring to a boil. In a small bowl, knead together the butter and flour. Whisk the butter mixture into the sauce, 1 tsp at a time, and continue whisking until the sauce returns to a boil and is thickened to your liking. Season with salt and pepper and stir in the parsley. Carve the meat and serve with the sauce on the side.

SLOW COOKER SAVVY

If chuck roast isn't available, brisket is another choice that works well here.

Bolito Misto with Salsa Verde

2 large sweet yellow onions, such as Vidalia, thinly sliced

3 medium carrots, cut into 1-in/2.5-cm lengths

Salt

Freshly ground black pepper

¼ tsp freshly grated nutmeg

2 tsp finely chopped fresh rosemary

One 4-lb/1.8-kg flat-cut beef brisket

2 tbsp extra-virgin olive oil

1 lb/455 g sweet Italian sausage

4 chicken legs, skin removed

4 garlic cloves, minced

4 cups/960 ml beef broth

¼ cup/60 ml demi-glace or soup base

¼ cup/15 g finely chopped fresh flat-leaf parsley

Salsa Verde (facing page), for serving

Elegant restaurants in Lombardy pride themselves on serving a stellar *bolito misto*, which means "mixed meat boil." Some restaurants actually have a rolling trolley that carries the ingredients to the table, with separate compartments to hold the different meats and the broth. *Bolito misto* traditionally has seven meats and seven vegetables, and is often served with salsa verde, a garlicky green sauce. Sometimes the meat is accompanied by a *mostarda*, which is a combination of fruits and mustard seeds, almost like a chutney, which gives the dish a lot of character and flavor.

This mixed boil contains Italian sausage and chicken, as well as the beef. I recommend adding a demi-glace or soup base to the broth, to enrich and deepen the flavor. I love to save the broth and use it to serve *tortellini en brodo*, another specialty of the area. You will need a 6- to 7-qt/5.5- to 6.5-L slow cooker to make this. If yours is smaller, halve the ingredients and cook for 8 hours on low.

Lay the onions and carrots in the bottom of a 6- to 7-qt/5.5- to 6.5-L slow cooker. In a small bowl, combine 2 tsp salt, 1 tsp pepper, the nutmeg, and rosemary and rub the mixture into the beef. In a large skillet, heat the olive oil over medium-high heat, and brown the beef on all sides. Transfer the meat to the slow cooker. Add the sausage to the skillet, brown all over, and transfer to the slow cooker. Brown the chicken on all sides in the skillet, and transfer to the slow cooker. Add the garlic and broth to the skillet and bring the broth to a boil, scraping up any browned bits on the bottom of the pan. Transfer the contents of the pan to the slow cooker, and add the demi-glace. Cover the slow cooker and cook on low for 10 hours, until the meats are cooked through and fork-tender.

When the meats are done, carefully remove them from the broth with tongs or a slotted spoon, and transfer to a cutting board or serving platter. Cover with aluminum foil. Skim off any excess fat from the broth, taste for seasoning, and add salt or pepper if needed. Add the parsley to the broth, cover, and set the slow cooker on the warm setting to keep warm. After the beef has rested for 10 minutes, slice into serving pieces, and arrange the chicken and sausage around the beef. Serve the meats in shallow bowls, with some of the broth, and pass the salsa verde on the side.

Salsa Verde

MAKES 2 CUPS/480 ML

This pestolike sauce made with fresh parsley and piquant capers is a terrific complement to Bolito Misto as well as grilled beef, poultry, or seafood. And it makes a delicious spread for panini.

2 cups/120 g packed fresh flat-leaf parsley

2 garlic cloves, minced

Pinch of red pepper flakes

½ cup/50 g capers, drained

2 tbsp finely chopped onion

½ tsp salt

½ cup/120 ml extra-virgin olive oil, plus 2 to 3 tbsp to float on top

In a food processor or blender, combine the parsley, garlic, red pepper flakes, capers, onion, and salt. Pulse on and off to break up the garlic and parsley. With the machine running, slowly pour in the ½ cup/120 ml olive oil, processing or blending until the mixture begins to come together. Transfer as much as you would like to a small serving bowl. Store the rest in an airtight container in the refrigerator for up to 1 week, and float the remaining olive oil on the top to prevent discoloration. May also be frozen for up to 1 month.

Short Ribs Bourguignon

4 tbsp/60 ml extra-virgin olive oil

3 cups/720 ml full-bodied red wine, such as French Burgundy, Merlot, Zinfandel, or Chianti (see Slow Cooker Savvy)

2 medium shallots, coarsely chopped

4 garlic cloves, minced

1 tsp dried thyme

2 bay leaves

1½ tsp salt

½ tsp freshly ground black pepper

4 lb/1.8 kg beef short ribs
(see Slow Cooker Savvy)

3 tbsp beef soup base or demi-glace
(see Slow Cooker Savvy)

2 large onions, coarsely chopped

2 to 4 tbsp unsalted butter, softened

¼ lb/115 g pearl onions, peeled

1 lb/455 g cremini mushrooms, quartered

2 tbsp all-purpose flour (optional)

Meaty short ribs replace stew meat in this riff on the French classic *boeuf bourguignonne*. The resulting dish yields fork-tender meat falling off the bones, in a rich sauce thickened naturally by the marrow from the bones. The secret to a tasty bourguignon in the slow cooker is to marinate the meat overnight, and then brown the meat and add it to the slow cooker in the morning. A long, lazy simmer for 10 hours, and a bit of finishing, and you have the stew that Julia Child called "one of the most delicious beef dishes concocted by man." I would agree. Serve the stew with Yukon gold potatoes mashed with Boursin cheese, or wide egg noodles to soak up the beefy, wine-flavored sauce.

In a large bowl, whisk together 2 tbsp of the olive oil, the wine, shallots, garlic, thyme, bay leaves, salt, and pepper. Put the short ribs in an extra-large zipper-top plastic bag, and pour the marinade over the ribs. Seal the bag and refrigerate for at least 8 hours, and up to 24 hours.

Strain the marinade into a small saucepan, and bring to a boil. Add the soup base to the marinade and set aside. In a large skillet, heat the remaining 2 tbsp olive oil, and brown the short ribs, a few at a time, transferring them to the insert of a 4- to 6-qt/3.5- to 5.5-L slow cooker when they're done. Sauté the onion for 3 to 4 minutes until it begins to soften. Pour the marinade into the skillet and bring to a boil, scraping up the browned bits on the bottom of the pan. Transfer the marinade to the slow cooker insert. Cover and cook on low for 10 hours, or on high for 5 hours, until the meat is tender.

Transfer the meat to a platter, and cover with aluminum foil to keep warm. Pour the sauce into a fat separator, or skim the fat from the surface and set aside.

In a large skillet, heat 2 tbsp of the butter over medium-high heat, and cook the pearl onions for 2 to 3 minutes, until fragrant. Add the mushrooms and sauté until the mushrooms turn golden. Add the sauce to the pearl onions and mushrooms and bring to a boil. If you think the sauce is thick enough, return it to the slow cooker along with the short ribs. Otherwise, in a small bowl, knead together the remaining 2 tbsp butter and the flour. Whisk the butter mixture into the sauce, 1 tsp at a time, and continue whisking until the sauce returns to a boil and is smooth and thickened to your liking. Return the sauce and the short ribs to the slow cooker and keep on the warm setting until you are ready to serve.

The type of wine you use here makes all the difference in the world. Wine that has too much tannin, such as Cabernet Sauvignon, will give the stew a wine-y flavor. A Cabernet blend will work, however.

If you can't find short ribs, cut up a chuck or shoulder roast into 2-in/5-cm pieces, trimming the fat.

Use a soup base or a demi-glace rather than stock or broth because the meat will render a lot of liquid, and if you add still more, it will become watered down.

Veal Osso Buco

SERVES 6

This world-famous dish is often served at elegant tables in Milan on a bed of risotto. A special spoon is provided so the diner can remove the marrow from the shank bone. Veal shanks become meltingly tender as they braise with aromatic vegetables in a tomato-based sauce scented with sage. The finishing touch to osso buco is a piquant garnish of citrus zest, garlic, and parsley—called *gremolata*—which gives the long-simmered dish a fresh and tangy finish.

In a large skillet, melt the butter over medium-high heat, and sauté the onion, celery, carrots, 2 garlic cloves, and sage for 3 minutes, or until the onion begins to soften. Transfer the contents of the skillet to the insert of a 5- to 7-qt/4.5- to 6.5-L slow cooker. Stir in the demi-glace and tomatoes. Turn the slow cooker to high and cover while you sauté the veal.

Tie the veal shanks with butcher's twine or silicone loops at 1-in/2.5-cm intervals to keep the meat close to the bones. In a shallow dish, mix together the flour, salt, and pepper. Dredge the veal in the flour mixture. In the same skillet, heat the olive oil over medium-high heat, and brown the meat on all sides in batches, turning frequently. When the meat is browned, add it to the sauce in the slow cooker. Pour the white wine into the skillet and bring to a boil, scraping up any browned bits on the bottom of the pan. Transfer to the slow cooker and stir the sauce. Cover and cook on high for 4 hours, or on low for 8 to 10 hours, until the veal is tender.

While the veal is cooking, in a small bowl, combine the remaining 3 garlic cloves, orange and lemon zest, and parsley. Cover with plastic wrap and set aside until the veal is ready to serve.

Skim any excess fat from the sauce. To serve the osso buco, remove the twine, and serve one shank per person with some of the sauce spooned over the top. Sprinkle with the gremolata. If you are serving the osso buco from the slow cooker as a buffet dish, stir the gremolata into the sauce before serving.

VARIATIONS

Quick Osso Buco

Substitute 3 lb/1.4 kg of veal shoulder, cut into 1-in/2.5-cm pieces, for the veal shanks. The sauce for this dish will not thicken naturally, so to help it along, in a small bowl, knead together 2 tbsp softened butter and 2 tbsp all-purpose flour. Whisk the butter mixture, 1 tsp at a time, into the sauce and continue whisking until the sauce returns to a boil and is smooth and thickened to your liking. Veal chunks will cook for 3 hours on high; 5 to 6 hours on low.

---

2 tbsp unsalted butter

1 large sweet yellow onion, such as Vidalia, finely chopped

3 ribs celery, including the leaves, finely chopped

3 medium carrots, finely chopped

5 garlic cloves, minced

6 fresh sage leaves, finely chopped

1½ cups/360 ml reconstituted veal demi-glace, or 1 cup/240 ml chicken broth

One 14½- to 15-oz/415- to 430-g can chopped tomatoes, with their juice

Six to eight ¾- to 1-lb/340-to 455-g veal shanks (about 6 lb/2.7 kg total)

½ cup/65 g all-purpose flour

1½ tsp salt

½ tsp freshly ground black pepper

3 tbsp extra-virgin olive oil

½ cup/120 ml dry white wine, such as Pinot Grigio or Sauvignon Blanc, or dry vermouth

Grated zest of 2 oranges

Grated zest of 1 lemon

1 cup/60 g finely chopped fresh flat-leaf parsley

Braised Veal with Forty Cloves of Garlic

3 lb/1.4 kg veal, either shoulder or shank, cut into 1-in/2.5-cm pieces

Salt

Freshly ground black pepper

3 tbsp extra-virgin olive oil

2 tsp dried tarragon

1 cup/240 ml full-bodied red wine, such as Burgundy, Merlot, or Zinfandel

One 14½- to 15-oz/415- to 430-g can tomato purée

1 cup/240 ml chicken broth

½ cup/120 ml beef broth

1 bay leaf

40 garlic cloves, peeled

2 tbsp unsalted butter, softened

2 tbsp all-purpose flour

½ cup/30 g finely chopped fresh flat-leaf parsley, for garnish

When James Beard's cookbook *Beard on Food* was published in 1974, readers were stunned by one of the recipes—a French Provençal chicken dish made with forty cloves of garlic. Beard knew the garlic would mellow over the long cooking time. But since chicken can dry out in a slow cooker, this version is made with veal, ensuring tender and succulent pieces of meat. With its tarragon-flavored tomato sauce, this dish is delicious served over rice, Boursin mashed potatoes, or buttered noodles.

Sprinkle the veal with 1½ tsp salt and ½ tsp pepper. Heat the olive oil in a large skillet over medium-high heat and sauté the veal, a few pieces at a time, until browned on all sides. Transfer the veal to the insert of a 5- to 7-qt/4.5- to 6.5-L slow cooker. Add the tarragon and wine to the skillet and bring to a boil, scraping up any browned bits on the bottom of the pan. Stir in the tomato purée, and transfer the mixture to the slow cooker. Stir in the chicken broth and beef broth, and add the bay leaf and garlic, stirring to distribute the ingredients. Cover and cook the veal on low for 6 to 7 hours, until it is tender.

Using a slotted spoon, transfer the veal to a serving bowl. Discard the bay leaf, and transfer the sauce to a large saucepan. Using a potato masher or immersion blender, mash or purée the garlic cloves. Bring the sauce to a boil. In a small bowl, knead together the butter and flour. Whisk the butter mixture into the sauce, 1 tsp at a time, and continue whisking until the sauce returns to a boil and is smooth and thickened to your liking. Taste the sauce for seasoning and add salt or pepper if needed. Return the veal and sauce to the cooker, garnish with the parsley, and serve.

Turkish Beef and Veal Meatballs

SERVES 6

These meatballs are a riff on *doner kebab*, the street food served in Turkey and around the Middle East, where it's also called *shawarma*. A meat mixture, cooked on a vertical spit, is sliced off and tucked into bread or served over pilaf, with salad. This version is made with beef and veal and is flavored with onion, garlic, rosemary, and oregano. The meat simmers in an untraditional but tasty red wine and beef broth sauce.

In a large mixing bowl, stir together the beef, veal, garlic, onion, oregano, rosemary, bread, milk, salt, pepper, lemon zest, and parsley until well combined. Form the meat mixture into 1½-in/4-cm balls, using a portion scoop. Combine the broth and wine in the insert of a 5- to 7-qt/4.5- to 6.5-L slow cooker. Drop the meatballs into the liquid. Cover the slow cooker and cook for 4 hours on high, or 6 to 7 hours on low.

Remove the meatballs from the slow cooker with a slotted spoon and transfer to a serving bowl. Sauce is optional. If you would like to accompany the meatballs with a sauce, boil the cooking liquid on the stove top for 10 minutes, and then spoon it over the meatballs. Or, to thicken the sauce even more, in a small bowl, knead together the butter and the flour. Whisk in the butter mixture, 1 tsp at a time, and continue whisking until the sauce returns to a boil and is smooth and thickened to your liking. Serve immediately.

◆❌ VARIATION ❌◆ Greek Gyro with Tzatziki Sauce

For a Greek twist, I like to tuck the meatballs into pita bread and serve them with a cucumber yogurt sauce, called tzatziki. To make the tzatziki, in a mixing bowl, whisk together 2 cups/480 ml Greek-style yogurt, 1 tbsp fresh lemon juice, 1 tbsp distilled white vinegar, 2 minced garlic cloves, 3 tbsp chopped fresh dill, 2 tsp salt, and ½ tsp freshly ground black pepper. Fold in 1 diced European cucumber, cover, and refrigerate for at least 2 hours, and up to 36 hours. To serve, place a few meatballs in a pita bread pocket and spoon some tzatziki sauce over the meatballs.

1½ lb/680 g lean ground beef

1 lb/455 g ground veal

2 garlic cloves, minced

½ cup/80 g finely chopped onion

2 tsp dried oregano

1 tsp dried rosemary, crushed in the palm of your hand

2 slices sturdy white bread, crust removed, and torn into pieces

¼ cup/60 ml milk

2 tsp salt

1 tsp freshly ground black pepper

Grated zest of 1 lemon

½ cup/30 g finely chopped fresh flat-leaf parsley

2 cups/480 ml beef broth

2 cup/480 ml full-bodied red wine, such as Burgundy, Merlot, or Zinfandel

2 tbsp unsalted butter, softened (optional)

2 tbsp all-purpose flour (optional)

Two Big Italian Meatballs

1 recipe Basic Marinara Sauce (page 176)

½ cup/120 ml milk

1½ cups/85 g fresh bread crumbs

1½ lb/680 g ground beef

½ lb/225 g lean ground pork

1 cup/160 g finely chopped onion

1 garlic clove, minced

Grated zest of 1 lemon

⅔ cup/75 g freshly grated pecorino romano cheese

1 tsp salt

½ tsp freshly ground black pepper

⅛ tsp freshly grated nutmeg

¼ cup/15 g finely chopped fresh flat-leaf parsley

1 large egg, lightly beaten

I call this recipe *Polpettoni alla Sorrella* in Italian. *Polpette* is the Italian word for "meatballs." *Polpettoni* are meat loaves made from the same type of meat, cheese, and bread crumb mixture. They're braised in a wine- or tomato-based sauce, and sliced before serving (as a main course). This recipe is inspired by my *sorella* (sister), Daniela Angelini, whose hospitality and graciousness have made me feel at home in her small village of Spello in Umbria. The *polpettoni* are delicious served over pasta, polenta, or rice, and they make a killer sandwich the next day!

Pour the marinara into the insert of a 5- to 7-qt/4.5- to 6.5-L slow cooker, cover, and set the slow cooker to low.

In a small bowl, pour the milk over the bread crumbs, and allow the bread to soak up the milk while you assemble the other ingredients.

In a large mixing bowl, combine the beef, pork, onion, garlic, lemon zest, cheese, salt, pepper, nutmeg, and parsley. Add the bread crumbs and milk and the egg and stir until blended. Form the meat into two loaves, each 6 to 8 in/15 to 20 cm long and 3 in/7.5 cm wide, and transfer to the insert. Cook on low for 5 hours, or on high for 2½ hours, until an instant-read meat thermometer inserted into the meat registers 170°F/77°C.

Using a large spatula, transfer the meat to a serving platter, and cover loosely with aluminum foil. Skim off the excess fat from the sauce. After the *polpettoni* have rested for 10 minutes, slice them ½ in/12 mm thick. Serve the meatballs napped with some of the marinara sauce.

Meatballs Languedoc

FOR THE SAUCE

2 tbsp extra-virgin olive oil

6 strips thick-cut bacon, finely chopped

1 large onion, finely chopped

6 saffron threads, crushed in the palm of your hand

Pinch of hot paprika

2 cups/480 ml chicken broth

Two 28- to 32-oz/800- to 910-g cans chopped tomatoes, with their juice

FOR THE MEATBALLS

1 lb/455 g lean ground pork

½ lb/225 g ground veal

4 garlic cloves, minced

2 tsp salt

1 tsp freshly ground black pepper

1 large egg, lightly beaten

Cooked noodles, potatoes, or polenta, for serving

½ cup/30 g finely chopped fresh flat-leaf parsley

This recipe hails from the French province of Languedoc-Roussillon, which borders Spain. The Spanish influence is certainly evident in these delicious meatballs, which are made from pork and veal and braise in a tomato sauce flavored with saffron and lardons (crispy pieces of bacon). Serve these with lots of crusty bread for dipping.

TO MAKE THE SAUCE / In a large skillet, heat the olive oil over medium-high heat and sauté the bacon until crisp. Drain all but 1 tbsp of the oil and add the onion, saffron, and paprika. Sauté for another 3 minutes, or until the onion begins to soften. Stir in the broth and bring to a boil, scraping up any browned bits on the bottom of the pan. Add the contents of the skillet to the insert of a 5- to 7-qt/4.5- to 6.5-L slow cooker. Stir in the tomatoes, cover the slow cooker, and cook on high while making the meatballs.

TO MAKE THE MEATBALLS / In a large mixing bowl, stir together the pork, veal, garlic, salt, and pepper. Stir in the egg to bind the mixture. Using a small portion scoop, roll the balls into 1-in/2.5-cm portions.

Drop the meatballs into the sauce, and cook on high for 3 hours, or on low for 5 to 6 hours, or until an instant-read meat thermometer inserted into a meatball registers 170°F/77°C.

Skim off any excess fat from the sauce. Serve the meatballs over noodles, potatoes, or polenta, sprinkled with the parsley.

Bolognese Sauce

Bologna is home to many culinary riches in the north-central region of Italy, but Bolognese sauce has to be one of my favorites. It's made with milk and cream to give it richness, along with ground pork, veal, and tomatoes. Although the recipe makes quite a bit, it freezes beautifully into 2-cup/480-ml packages; each one will sauce 1 lb/455 g of pasta nicely. Bolognese is the basis for Lasagna Bolognese (page 130), and is frequently ladled over tortellini, another specialty of the region.

In a large skillet, melt the butter with the olive oil over medium-high heat and add the onion, carrots, celery, and garlic. Sauté until the vegetables are softened. Add the pork and veal and sauté until the meats are no longer pink in color, breaking up any large chunks with a wooden spoon. Spoon off any excess fat or water so the pan is dry. Add the nutmeg and cinnamon and sauté for another 2 minutes, to allow the flavors to blend.

Add the milk and cream, bring the mixture to a boil, and cook until the milk and cream have just about evaporated. Transfer the mixture to the insert of a 5- to 7-qt/4.5- to 6.5-L slow cooker, add the wine and tomatoes, and stir to blend. Cover and cook the sauce on high for 6 to 7 hours, until the sauce is thickened.

Taste for seasoning and adjust by adding salt and pepper. Serve some of the sauce immediately over al dente pasta, and store the rest in airtight containers in the freezer.

1 tbsp unsalted butter

2 tbsp olive oil

1 large sweet yellow onion, such as Vidalia, finely chopped

1 cup/100 g finely diced carrots

1 cup/100 g finely diced celery

1 garlic clove, minced

1½ lb/680 g lean ground pork

1 lb/455 g ground veal

⅛ tsp freshly grated nutmeg

⅛ tsp ground cinnamon

½ cup/120 ml whole milk

½ cup/120 ml heavy cream

1 cup/240 ml dry white wine, such as Pinot Grigio or Sauvignon Blanc, or dry vermouth

Two 28- to 32-oz/800- to 910-g cans crushed plum tomatoes (San Marzano are best)

Salt

Freshly ground black pepper

Pappardelle, tortellini, or another pasta, cooked until al dente, for serving

POULTRY
(CHICKEN, DUCK, GAME HENS, AND TURKEY)

Poultry served in the Mediterranean is always highly flavored, tender, and delicious. The flavor palate runs wild, from chicken stuffed with Serrano ham and Manchego cheese (page 84), to a duck tagine with dates and dried apricots (page 90). Turkey, game hens, duck, and the barnyard chicken are all elevated to five-star status when cooked in your slow cooker, yielding tender, juicy meat with Mediterranean flavors— surefire winners for your dinner table.

For most recipes, I advise you to remove the skin from the poultry before cooking in the slow cooker. The skin adds fat, and it will also buckle around the meat, making it difficult to serve. I like boneless cuts in many cases since the meat does fall off the bone at the end of the cooking time. Stuffed chicken breasts, which can become dry and tasteless in the oven, emerge succulent, juicy, and infused with the saucy flavors added to the cooker, giving you a great meal to serve to special friends and family.

Chicken Tagine with Preserved Lemons and Olives

4 tbsp/60 ml extra-virgin olive oil

2 large onions, thinly sliced

1 tsp saffron threads, crushed in the palm of your hand

1 tsp sweet paprika

1 tsp ground coriander

¼ tsp ground ginger

4 drops Tabasco or your favorite hot sauce

4 lb/1.8 kg bone-in chicken pieces (such as 3 leg quarters and 3 breast quarters), skin removed

1½ cups/360 ml chicken broth

2 tbsp fresh lemon juice

1½ cups/180 g pitted picholine or other green olives

¼ cup/30 g finely chopped preserved lemon rind (see Slow Cooker Savvy)

½ cup/30 g finely chopped fresh cilantro

Salt (optional)

Freshly ground black pepper (optional)

Cooked rice or couscous, or flatbreads such as pita, for serving

A tagine is a vessel with a conical top that is traditionally used in Morocco to slow-cook meat and spices into succulent bits. A dish produced in this cooking vessel is also called a tagine. A tagine typically contains preserved lemons, which are cured with salt. They can be found in Middle Eastern markets, packed in brine. Or you can make your own (see Slow Cooker Savvy). Green picholine olives give this dish a special flavor, but you can substitute your favorite type of green olive, should picholines not be available. Tagines are almost always served with a starch of some sort to soak up the scrumptious juices. Couscous, flatbread, or rice works well.

Heat 2 tbsp of the olive oil in a large skillet over medium-high heat, and sauté the onions, saffron, paprika, coriander, and ginger for 3 minutes, or until the onions begin to soften. Transfer the contents of the pan to the insert of a 5- to 7-qt/4.5- to 6.5-L slow cooker, and stir in the Tabasco sauce.

In the same skillet, heat the remaining 2 tbsp olive oil, and brown the chicken on all sides, a few pieces at a time, transferring the browned chicken to the slow-cooker insert. Pour the broth and lemon juice into the skillet, bring to a boil, and scrape up any browned bits on the bottom of the pan. Add the liquids to the slow-cooker insert. Cover the slow cooker and cook for 3 hours on high, or 5 to 6 hours on low.

Carefully remove the chicken from the slow cooker with tongs or a large spatula. Skim off any excess fat from the sauce, and stir in the olives, lemon rind, and cilantro. Taste for seasoning and add salt or pepper if needed. Return the chicken to the slow cooker. Serve the tagine from the slow cooker with rice, couscous, or flatbread.

SLOW COOKER SAVVY

Making your own preserved lemons is simple and satisfying. The quantity of lemons and salt you will need depends on the size of your jar. For a 2-qt/2-L jar, use about 5 to 6 medium lemons and ½ to 1 cup/105 to 205 g sea salt. Cut an end off each lemon and stand on its flat end and cut into quarters, leaving ½ in/12 mm still attached at the bottom. Push the lemons into the jar, and sprinkle with the salt. Push two 3-in/7.5-cm cinnamon sticks, 1 bay leaf, 5 whole cloves, and 5 black peppercorns into the jar. Pour in ½ cup/120 ml fresh lemon juice to cover the lemons. Seal the jar, and leave in a cool, dry place for 1 month. When ready to use, discard the flesh from a quarter, and chop the rind into small pieces. Store the opened jar in the refrigerator for up to 6 months.

Braised Basque Chicken

The Basque people live in the northeastern region of Spain and across the border in southwestern France. They are known worldwide for their cuisine, unique language—which resembles neither French nor Spanish—and culture. The Basque people pride themselves on keeping these traditions alive. They also believe in keeping their food simple (I love that!), and do not like to mask the flavors of their ingredients. This one is a typical Basque chicken dish (many of which are cooked in covered casseroles), made with onion, bell peppers, tomato, and a bit of ham. The slow cooker takes good care of the ingredients, and the result is succulent pieces of chicken steeped in the flavors in the pot.

Sprinkle the chicken with 1 tsp salt and ½ tsp pepper. In a large skillet, heat 2 tbsp of the olive oil over medium-high heat and brown the chicken on all sides, a few pieces at a time, being careful not to crowd the pan. Transfer the browned chicken to the insert of a 5- to 7-qt/4.5- to 6.5-L slow cooker.

Add the remaining 2 tbsp oil to the skillet and sauté the ham, letting it brown a bit. Transfer to the insert of the slow cooker. Add the onions, garlic, and bell peppers to the skillet, and season with 1 tsp salt and ½ tsp pepper. Cook until the onions begin to soften, about 3 minutes. Add the tomatoes to the skillet and bring to a boil, scraping up any browned bits on the bottom of the pan. Transfer the contents of the skillet to the insert of the slow cooker, covering the chicken with the mixture. Cover the slow cooker and cook on high for 3 hours, or on low for 5 to 6 hours, until the chicken is cooked through.

Skim off any excess fat on the sauce, taste for seasoning, and add salt or pepper if necessary. Serve the chicken garnished with the green and black olives and parsley.

---

3 lb/1.4 kg bone-in chicken pieces (3 leg quarters and 3 breast quarters work here), skin removed

Salt

Freshly ground black pepper

4 tbsp/60 ml extra-virgin olive oil

¼ lb/115 g Serrano ham, cut into ½-in/12-mm cubes

2 large onions, thinly sliced

2 garlic cloves, minced

2 medium red bell peppers, cored and cut into ½-in/12-mm strips

2 medium yellow bell peppers, cored and cut into ½-in/12-mm strips

One 28- to 32-oz/800- to 910-g can chopped tomatoes, with their juice

½ cup/60 g pitted picholine or other green olives, for garnish

½ cup/60 g pitted niçoise olives, for garnish

¼ cup/15 g finely chopped fresh flat-leaf parsley, for garnish

Chicken Hunter's Style

1 lb/455 g fingerling potatoes, scrubbed

4 tbsp/60 ml extra-virgin olive oil

2 tsp salt

1 tsp freshly ground black pepper

3 lb/1.4 kg bone-in chicken pieces (such as 3 breast quarters and 4 leg quarters), skin removed

4 slices pancetta, finely chopped

6 garlic cloves, sliced

1½ tbsp finely chopped fresh rosemary

⅔ cup/165 ml balsamic vinegar

½ cup/120 ml chicken broth

Cacciatore, loosely translated as "hunter's style," has come to mean chicken drowned in tomato sauce at red-sauce Italian restaurants. An Italian hunter wouldn't have a can of tomato sauce in his pouch. But he would have garlic, a bit of wine or vinegar, maybe some bacon or pancetta, and herbs picked in a nearby meadow for the dinner he would cook over an open fire. This dish could be made with whatever the hunter happened to catch that day: rabbit, pheasant, boar, or wild turkey. My *nonna*, Aleandra, would make this chicken, and it was all I could do to keep my fingers from pulling pieces of succulent chicken off the bone, right from the pan. In the slow cooker, the chicken is juicy, tender, and redolent of garlic, rosemary, and balsamic vinegar. It cooks along with a few fingerling potatoes, so all you need to finish off this meal is a green veggie or salad.

Arrange the potatoes in the insert of a 5- to 7-qt/4.5- to 6.5-L slow cooker. Sprinkle with 2 tbsp of the olive oil, and then 1 tsp of the salt and ½ tsp of the pepper. Stir the potatoes to coat them with the oil mixture. Sprinkle the chicken with the remaining 1 tsp salt and ½ tsp pepper and set aside.

In a large skillet, over high heat, sauté the pancetta in the remaining 2 tbsp olive oil until crisp and the fat is rendered. Add the chicken to the skillet, a few pieces at a time, and brown on all sides. Transfer the chicken to the insert of the slow cooker. Add the garlic and rosemary to the skillet, and cook for 2 minutes, until the garlic is fragrant and begins to soften. Add the vinegar and broth to the skillet and bring to a boil, scraping up any browned bits on the bottom of the pan. Pour the contents of the pan over the chicken. Cover the slow cooker and cook on high for 3 hours, or on low for 6 hours, until the chicken is cooked through.

Carefully remove the chicken from the slow cooker using tongs, and transfer to a serving platter. Arrange the potatoes around the chicken, spoon the sauce over both, and serve.

Saffron-Braised Chicken Thighs Stuffed with Serrano Ham

Boneless chicken thighs are readily available in your supermarket. Serve them with a bread stuffing made with salty Serrano ham, and a creamy, saffron-scented sauce, and your dining room will be transformed into an elegant Spanish restaurant. Similar to prosciutto, Serrano ham is salt-cured and then dry-aged. (Some people feel Serrano ham is superior in flavor because it's made from Iberian pigs.) If you can't find Serrano ham, prosciutto will work here.

Melt 2 tbsp of the butter with the olive oil in a large skillet over medium-high heat. Sauté the garlic and ham for 2 to 3 minutes, until the garlic is fragrant and the ham begins to soften. Transfer the mixture to a medium bowl, and stir in ¼ cup/ 15 g of the parsley, the bread crumbs, and cheese.

Spread out a chicken thigh on a cutting board shiny-side (skin-side) down. Sprinkle with salt and pepper, and mound 2 tbsp of the filling in the center of the chicken. Roll the chicken around the filling, and secure with a toothpick or silicone bands. Repeat with the remaining chicken and filling.

In the same skillet, melt another 2 tbsp butter and brown the chicken all over. Transfer to the insert of a 5- to 7-qt/4.5- to 6.5-L slow cooker. Add the saffron and wine to the skillet and bring to a boil, scraping up any browned bits on the bottom of the pan. Pour the wine mixture over the chicken and stir in the broth. Cover and cook 5 to 6 hours on low, until the chicken is cooked through.

While the chicken is cooking, allow the remaining 2 tbsp butter to soften. Carefully remove the chicken from the slow cooker using tongs, and transfer to a cutting board. Cover with aluminum foil and allow to rest for 5 to 10 minutes. Knead the softened butter and flour together in a small bowl. Pour the sauce from the cooker into a saucepan, and bring to a boil. Whisk in the butter mixture, 1 tsp at a time, and continue whisking until the sauce returns to a boil and is smooth and thickened to your liking. Stir in the remaining parsley, taste, and season with salt and pepper if necessary. Stir in the cream. Bring to serving temperature. Cut each chicken thigh into two pieces, and serve in a pool of the sauce.

6 tbsp/85 g unsalted butter

2 tbsp extra-virgin olive oil

2 garlic cloves, minced

3 thin slices Serrano ham, finely diced

½ cup/30 g finely chopped fresh flat-leaf parsley

2 cups/110 g fresh bread crumbs

½ cup/60 g finely grated Manchego cheese

8 boneless, skinless chicken thighs

Salt

Freshly ground black pepper

1 tsp saffron threads, crushed in the palm of your hand

½ cup/120 ml dry white wine, such as Pinot Grigio or Sauvignon Blanc, or dry vermouth

1½ cups/360 ml chicken broth

2 tbsp all-purpose flour

½ cup/120 ml heavy cream

Chicken Stuffed with Serrano Ham in a Creamy Onion Sauce

8 boneless, skinless chicken breast halves, tenders removed (see Slow Cooker Savvy)

8 thin slices Serrano ham

8 thin slices Manchego cheese

6 tbsp/85 g unsalted butter

1 tbsp extra-virgin olive oil

6 medium sweet yellow onions, such as Vidalia, thinly sliced

Salt

Freshly ground black pepper

2 tbsp sugar

½ cup/120 ml dry white wine, such as Pinot Grigio or Sauvignon Blanc, or dry vermouth

1 cup/250 ml chicken broth

2 bay leaves

1 cup/240 ml heavy cream

¼ cup/15 g finely chopped fresh flat-leaf parsley

Salty, slightly spicy, and sweetened with creamy caramelized onions, this dish is worthy of your next fiesta! Serrano ham is a salt-cured, aged ham from Spain. The onion sauce soaks up its flavor and gives the dish a lovely texture. Serve this over sautéed spinach, rice, pasta, or mashed potatoes for a special meal.

On a cutting board, spread out a piece of plastic wrap as large as the board. Trim the chicken breasts of any excess fat, and lay one breast shiny-side (skin-side) down on the plastic wrap. Place another piece of plastic wrap over the breast, and pound with a meat pounder, flat-bottom wine bottle, or rolling pin to an even thickness, about ½ in/12 mm. Repeat with the remaining chicken.

Lay a slice of ham over a chicken breast half, and cover with a slice of cheese. Roll up the chicken, beginning at the widest end and tucking in the sides. Secure with a toothpick or silicone bands. Repeat with the remaining chicken, ham, and cheese.

In a large skillet, over medium-high heat, melt the butter with the olive oil. Add the chicken breasts, a few at a time, and brown them all over. Transfer the browned chicken to the insert of a 5- to 7-qt/4.5- to 6.5-L slow cooker. Put the onions in the same skillet; sprinkle with 1½ tsp salt, 1 tsp pepper, and the sugar; and sauté over medium-high heat until the onions begin to turn golden. Add the wine and broth and bring to a boil, scraping up any browned bits on the bottom of the pan. Transfer the contents of the skillet to the slow-cooker insert, and add the bay leaves. Cover and cook for 2 hours on high, or 3½ to 4 hours on low. The onions should be practically melted into the sauce, and the chicken should register 160°F/71°C on an instant-read meat thermometer.

Using a slotted spoon, transfer the chicken to a cutting board, and cover with aluminum foil. Remove the bay leaves, pour the sauce into a saucepan, and bring to a boil. If you prefer a smooth sauce, using an immersion blender, purée the sauce. Either way, add the cream, return to a boil, and season with salt or pepper if needed. Stir in the parsley and keep warm.

Cut each chicken breast on the diagonal into three pieces. Serve the chicken in a pool of the sauce, or nap the chicken with some of the sauce on a serving platter, and serve with the rest of the sauce on the side.

SLOW COOKER SAVVY

The tender, or tenderloin, of the chicken breast is a small flap of meat under the breast. Sometimes the tender is attached to the breast, and other times it's missing. I recommend that you remove the tenders so the chicken breasts have a more uniform thickness and will cook more evenly. Store the tenders in the freezer, to use later for kebabs or chicken salad.

Spinach and Feta–Stuffed Chicken Breasts in Lemon-Dill Sauce

Emerging succulent, juicy, and flavored with salty feta, this chicken dish pairs well with rice, pasta, or mashed potatoes, which soak up the lemony dill-flecked sauce.

In a large skillet, melt 2 tbsp of the butter over medium-high heat, and sauté the shallot and garlic for 2 minutes, until the shallot is slightly softened. Add the spinach, 1 tsp salt, ½ tsp pepper, and the nutmeg to the skillet. Sauté the spinach until the liquid in the pan has evaporated and the spinach is dry. Remove from the heat, cool the mixture slightly, and stir in the feta cheese. Set aside.

On a cutting board, spread out a piece of plastic wrap as large as the board. Trim the chicken breasts of any excess fat, and lay one breast shiny-side (skin-side) down on the plastic wrap. Place another piece of plastic wrap over the breast, and pound with a meat pounder, flat-bottom wine bottle, or rolling pin to an even thickness, about ½ in/12 mm. Repeat with the remaining chicken.

Lay a chicken breast half on a flat surface and season with salt and pepper. Place about 2 tbsp of the filling in the center of the breast. Roll up the breast, beginning at the widest end and tucking in the sides, and secure with a toothpick or silicone bands. Repeat with the remaining chicken and filling.

Melt the remaining 2 tbsp butter in the skillet over medium-high heat, and brown the stuffed chicken breasts in batches, transferring them to the insert of a 5- to 7-qt/4.5- to 6.5-L slow cooker when they're done. Add the wine to the skillet, scraping up the browned bits on the bottom of the pan. Pour the wine and broth into the insert. Cover and cook for 2½ hours on high; 4 to 5 hours on low, until the chicken is cooked through and registers 160°F/71°C on an instant-read meat thermometer.

Using tongs, remove the chicken from the slow cooker, arrange on a cutting board, and cover with foil. Allow the chicken to rest for 5 minutes. Cut each chicken breast half on the diagonal into three pieces, and serve in a pool of the Lemon-Dill Sauce.

4 tbsp/55 g unsalted butter

2 tbsp finely chopped shallot

1 garlic clove, minced

One 1-lb/455-g package frozen spinach, defrosted and squeezed dry

Salt

Freshly ground black pepper

⅛ tsp freshly grated nutmeg

1 cup/120 g crumbled feta cheese

6 boneless, skinless chicken breast halves

½ cup/120 ml dry white wine, such as Pinot Grigio or Sauvignon Blanc, or dry vermouth

2 cups/480 ml chicken broth

Lemon-Dill Sauce (page 88), for serving

Lemon-Dill Sauce

MAKES ABOUT 3 CUPS

This is a great all-purpose sauce, reminiscent of hollandaise, but it can be made ahead of time. It's terrific with chicken, seafood, or vegetables.

2 tbsp unsalted butter

2 tbsp all-purpose flour

1½ cups/360 ml chicken broth (see Slow Cooker Savvy)

1 cup/240 ml heavy cream

Grated zest of 1 lemon

2 tbsp fresh lemon juice

¼ cup/15 g chopped fresh dill

Salt and freshly ground black pepper (optional)

In a medium saucepan, melt the butter over medium heat, and whisk in the flour. Cook, whisking constantly, and when white bubbles form on the surface, cook for another 2 to 3 minutes, still whisking. Gradually add the broth, whisking until it comes to a boil and the mixture is smooth and thickened.

Stir in the cream, lemon zest and juice, and dill. Season with salt and pepper if necessary. Serve immediately, or cool to room temperature and refrigerate for up to 4 days. Gently reheat over low heat before serving.

SLOW COOKER SAVVY

If you would like to use the pan juices from the main recipe, strain 1½ cups of the juices into a measuring cup and substitute them for the chicken broth.

Chicken Piccata

A one-hour slow cooker dinner is my kind of food! The chicken is bathed in a buttery sauce that is fragrant with lemon, garlic, and capers. It makes a great change of pace from ordinary grilled or roasted chicken. The zesty sauce is the perfect complement for a cheesy starch, such as fettucine Alfredo or risotto. Why make it in the slow cooker, you might ask. The slow cooker keeps the chicken moist and tender, which is more difficult to achieve if you cook chicken piccata in a skillet.

On a cutting board, spread out a piece of plastic wrap as large as the board. Trim the chicken breasts of any excess fat, and lay one breast shiny-side (skin-side) down on the plastic wrap. Place another piece of plastic wrap over the breast, and pound with a meat pounder, flat-bottom wine bottle, or rolling pin to an even thickness, about ½ in/12 mm. Repeat with the remaining chicken.

On a dinner plate, or in a large, shallow dish, combine the flour, 1 tsp salt, and ½ tsp pepper. In a large skillet, over medium-high heat, melt the butter with the olive oil. Dredge the chicken in the flour, and sauté on each side, until it turns white. Transfer the chicken to the insert of a 5-to 7-quart/4.5- to 6.5-L slow cooker as it is cooked. Add the garlic, lemon juice and zest, broth, paprika, and capers to the butter and oil in the skillet. Cook for 2 minutes, and then pour the mixture into the slow cooker. Cover and cook on high for 1 hour, or on low for 2 hours, until the chicken is cooked through.

Carefully remove the chicken from the slow cooker using tongs, arrange on a serving platter, and cover with aluminum foil. Pour the sauce into a saucepan, and bring to a boil. Taste for seasoning and add salt or pepper if necessary. Pour some of the sauce over the chicken and serve, passing the remaining sauce on the side.

8 boneless, skinless chicken breast halves, tenders removed (see Slow Cooker Savvy, page 85)

1 cup/130 g all-purpose flour

Salt

Freshly ground black pepper

4 tablespoons/55 g unsalted butter

½ cup/120 ml extra-virgin olive oil

8 garlic cloves, minced

⅔ cup/165 ml fresh lemon juice

Grated zest of 1 lemon

½ cup/120 ml chicken broth

1 tsp sweet paprika

1 cup/100 g capers packed in brine, drained

Duck Tagine with Dried Fruits

One 4-lb/1.8-kg duck, cut into serving pieces or quarters

1½ tsp salt

1 tsp freshly ground black pepper

4 tbsp/60 ml extra-virgin olive oil

3 large onions, coarsely chopped

2 garlic cloves, chopped

1 tsp ground cumin

½ tsp ground cinnamon

½ tsp ground ginger

Pinch of saffron threads, crushed in the palm of you hand

1 cup/240 ml chicken broth

1 cup/240 ml beef broth

1 cup/170 g pitted dates, quartered

1 cup/170 g dried apricots, quartered

¼ cup/15 g finely chopped fresh cilantro

Couscous (page 142), for serving

This tagine takes advantage of dried fruit for its flavors: The combination of apricots and dates gives a nice balance of sweet and tart, enhanced by the ginger and cinnamon in the rich sauce. Instead of the couscous, you can also serve this over fragrant basmati pilaf.

Sprinkle the duck pieces evenly with the salt and pepper, rubbing them into the duck. Heat 2 tbsp of the olive oil in a large skillet over medium-high heat and brown the duck, a few pieces at a time, transferring the browned meat to the insert of a 5- to 7-qt/4.5- to 6.5-L slow cooker. Add the remaining 2 tbsp olive oil to the skillet and sauté the onions, garlic, cumin, cinnamon, ginger, and saffron until the onions begin to soften, about 3 minutes. Pour in the chicken broth, bring to a boil, and scrape up any browned bits on the bottom of the pan. Transfer the contents of the skillet to the slow cooker, and add the beef broth, dates, and apricots. Cover and cook on low for 6 to 7 hours, until the duck is tender.

Using tongs or a large spatula, transfer the duck to a serving platter and cover with aluminum foil. Skim off any excess fat from the sauce, stir in the cilantro, and return the duck to the cooker. Serve with couscous.

Duck Confit

The prize of the Périgord region of southwestern France, duck confit is slow-cooked in duck fat and preserved in the same fat. The preparation is sometimes a laborious process for the home cook, but the slow cooker takes care of the work, so you can enjoy the day. The duck can be removed from the fat and shredded to use in salads and other dishes. My favorite way to prepare it is to roast the confit briefly in a hot oven, which yields crispy skin (my favorite part!) and tender meat. Serve the duck with Sarlat potatoes, which are fried in duck fat!

6 duck legs (about 3 lb/1.4 kg total)

4 garlic cloves, minced

2 tbsp salt

2 tsp freshly ground black pepper

1 tbsp herbes de Provence (see Slow Cooker Savvy, page 114)

3 lb/1.4 kg duck fat (see Slow Cooker Savvy)

Rinse the duck legs in cold water and pat dry. In a small bowl, mix together the garlic, salt, pepper, and herbes de Provence to make a paste and rub half of the mixture into the duck. Cover the duck legs and the remaining rub and refrigerate overnight.

Melt the duck fat in the insert of a 5- to 7-qt/4.5- to 6.5-L slow cooker on low and stir in the remaining rub. Rinse the duck legs in cold water, pat dry, and add to the fat. Cook on low for 6 to 8 hours, until the duck is cooked through and tender.

Carefully transfer the duck legs to a platter, and cover with aluminum foil. Allow the fat to cool slightly, and strain through cheesecloth into a large airtight container. Submerge the duck legs in the fat and let cool. Refrigerate until the fat congeals, or up to 1 month.

To warm the confit and crisp the skin, preheat the oven to 400°F/200°C/gas 6. Remove the legs from the fat, scraping any excess back into the container. Place the legs on a rack in a roasting pan, and bake for 15 to 20 minutes, until the skin is crispy. If the skin still isn't crisped to your liking, run it under the broiler for 5 to 7 minutes. Serve immedaitely.

❈ SLOW COOKER SAVVY ❈

Duck is becoming more readily available in markets, but if you are having a hard time finding duck or duck fat, D'Artagnan sells high-quality duck fat and ducks online (see Resources, page 184).

Duck confit should be cooked only on low and only in a good-quality slow cooker. Inexpensive slow cookers run hotter and will burn the fat, giving it a rancid odor and flavor. The fat should only bubble around the edges of the pan, and not be at a rolling boil.

Duck Cassoulet

SERVES 6 TO 8

Cassoulet is a hearty winter dish from the southwestern region of France. There is much discussion about the ingredients necessary for a proper cassoulet, but the flavors depend on the cook and the region in which it's prepared. In the Languedoc area of Castelnaudary, cassoulet is a pig fest, featuring sausages, pork, and ham, as well large white beans. Here, I've called for duck legs for an added dimension of flavor. It's a grand recipe to make in the slow cooker, a delicious one-pot party dish to serve when it's cold outside. You will need a 6- to 7-qt/5.5- to 6.5-L slow cooker for this meal. Start this dish the night before so the beans have time to cook.

~~~~~~

In a colander, rinse the beans in cold water, picking them over and discarding any broken beans, stones, or dirt. Put the beans in a large bowl and add enough water to cover by at least 2 in/5 cm. Cover with plastic wrap and allow to soak overnight. When ready to use, rinse the beans thoroughly and set aside.

In a large skillet, heat 2 tbsp of the olive oil over medium-high heat, and sauté the bacon until it is crisp. Transfer to the insert of a 6- to 7-qt/5.5- to 6.5-L slow cooker. Add the sausage to the skillet and render some of its fat, transferring it to the insert of the slow cooker when browned. Brown the pork shoulder in the skillet, a few pieces at a time, transferring them to the slow cooker when done. Brown the duck legs on all sides, and add to the slow cooker. Turn the slow cooker to low and cover.

In the same skillet, sauté the onions, two-thirds of the garlic, the thyme, and bay leaves for 5 minutes, or until the onions become softened. Add the tomatoes and wine and bring to a boil, scraping up any browned bits on the bottom of the pan. Transfer the contents of the skillet to the slow cooker, and slowly pour in the broths and demi-glace. Distribute the beans evenly throughout the cassoulet. Cover and cook on low for 12 to 14 hours.

Meanwhile, preheat the oven to 350°F/180°C/gas 4 and line a baking sheet with a silicone baking liner or parchment paper. In a large mixing bowl, combine the bread crumbs, cheese, remaining garlic, ¼ cup/15 g of the parsley, and the remaining ¼ cup/60 ml oil. Spread out the crumb mixture on the baking sheet and bake for 10 to 15 minutes, until the crumbs are golden brown. Remove from the oven and cool.

CONTINUED /

1 lb/455 g dried large white beans

6 tbsp/90 ml extra-virgin olive oil

8 strips thick-cut bacon, cut into 1-in/2.5-cm pieces

1½ lb/680 g kielbasa (smoked Polish sausage), cut into rounds

2½ lb/1.2 kg pork shoulder, excess fat trimmed, and cut into 1-in/2.5-cm pieces

4 duck legs, skin and any excess fat removed

2 large onions, finely chopped

6 garlic cloves, minced

4 sprigs fresh thyme

2 bay leaves

One 28- to 32-oz/800- to 910-g can chopped tomatoes, with their juice

1½ cups/360 ml dry white wine, such as Pinot Grigio or Sauvignon Blanc, or dry vermouth

4 cups/960 ml chicken broth

2 cups/480 ml beef broth

¼ cup/60 ml demi-glace or soup base

1½ cups/85 g fresh bread crumbs

½ cup/60 g finely grated Parmigiano-Reggiano cheese

½ cup/30 g finely chopped fresh flat-leaf parsley

Salt (optional)

Freshly ground black pepper (optional)

POULTRY ❋ 93

When the cassoulet is finished, the duck should be tender, the pork falling apart, and the beans creamy. Skim off any excess fat from the sauce and remove the bay leaves. Taste the sauce, add salt and pepper if needed, and the remaining ¼ cup/15 g parsley. Sprinkle the toasted bread crumbs over the cassoulet and serve.

✻ SLOW COOKER SAVVY ✻

You can make the crumb topping in advance and store in a zipper-top plastic bag at room temperature for up to 2 days, or freeze for up to 2 months.

If you have a slow-cooker insert that is safe under the broiler (check your manufacturer's instructions), you can slide the cassoulet under the broiler to brown the crumb topping instead of toasting the crumbs in the oven.

Braised Duck Legs with Wild Mushrooms and Almonds

Duck is luxurious, a treat for those of us who love to eat it. That said, make this dish when you know that your guests feel the same way. And seek out some exotic mushrooms for this dish; they enhance the finished sauce. Emerging succulent, juicy, and full of flavor from the slow cooker, the duck is delicious served with rice or buttered noodles. The veal demi-glace enriches the mushroom-studded sauce.

Lay the duck on a cutting board, and sprinkle evenly with the salt, pepper, and thyme, rubbing them into the duck. In a large skillet, heat the olive oil over medium-high heat and brown the duck on all sides, a few pieces at a time, turning frequently. Transfer the browned meat to the insert of a 5- to 7-qt/4.5- to 6.5-L slow cooker. Add the shallots to the skillet, and sauté for 3 minutes, or until they begin to soften. Add the mushrooms and sauté for 3 minutes to release some liquid. Stir in the Madeira, bring to a boil, and scrape up any browned bits on the bottom of the pan. Transfer the mixture to the slow cooker, and add the demi-glace and bay leaf. Cover the slow cooker and cook on low for 5 hours, until the duck is tender and registers 160°F/71°C on an instant-read meat thermometer.

Using tongs or a large spatula, transfer the duck to a serving platter and cover with aluminum foil. Pour the mushroom sauce into a large saucepan, remove the bay leaf, and bring to a boil. Knead the butter with the flour in a small bowl. Whisk into the sauce, 1 tsp at a time, and continue whisking until the sauce returns to a boil and is thickened to your liking. Stir in the parsley and the almonds and pour some of the sauce over the duck on the serving platter. Serve the duck with the remaining sauce on the side.

6 duck legs (about 5 to 6 lb/2.3 to 2.7 kg total), skin removed

2 tsp salt

1 tsp freshly ground black pepper

1 tsp dried thyme

¼ cup/60 ml extra-virgin olive oil

1 cup/160 g finely chopped shallots

1½ lb/680 g mixed mushrooms, such as chanterelles, oyster, cremini, shiitake, lobster, morel, and hen of the woods, in any combination

½ cup/120 ml Madeira wine

2 cups/480 ml veal demi-glace

1 bay leaf

2 tbsp unsalted butter, softened

2 tbsp all-purpose flour

½ cup/30 g finely chopped fresh flat-leaf parsley

½ cup/55 g toasted sliced almonds

Game Hens Braised with Coriander and Apricot Rice Stuffing

SERVES 6

FOR THE SAUCE

2 tbsp unsalted butter

¼ cup/40 g finely chopped shallots

1 tsp sweet paprika

1 tsp saffron threads, crushed in the palm of your hand

2 tbsp all-purpose flour

1½ cups/360 ml chicken broth

½ cup/120 ml apricot nectar

2 tbsp fresh lemon juice

1 cup/170 g coarsely chopped dried apricots

FOR THE STUFFING AND HENS

2 tbsp extra-virgin olive oil

½ cup/80 g finely chopped sweet yellow onion, such as Vidalia

1 tsp coriander seeds

½ cup/85 g finely chopped dried apricots

2 cups/430 g cooked basmati rice

1 large egg

Six 1-lb/455-g Cornish game hens

Salt

Freshly ground black pepper

2 tbsp cornstarch mixed with 2 tbsp water

½ cup/30 g finely chopped fresh cilantro

The rice stuffing contains coriander seeds, which were found in the tomb of King Tutankhamen, and were mentioned in the biblical story of the exodus of the Jews from Egypt. According to the Bible, coriander seeds flavored the manna from heaven, which the Jews ate while traveling in the desert. Fragrant and strong, coriander pairs well with the dried apricots and rice and gives the game hen meat a smoky quality.

TO MAKE THE SAUCE / In a small saucepan, over medium-high heat, melt the butter and sauté the shallots, paprika, and saffron for 3 minutes, or until the shallots begin to soften. Add the flour and sauté for another 2 to 3 minutes, until the flour is cooked. Slowly add the broth, apricot nectar, and lemon juice and bring the liquid to a boil. Stir in the apricots and transfer the mixture to the insert of a 5- to 7-qt/4.5- to 6.5-L slow cooker. Cover and turn the slow cooker on low.

TO MAKE THE STUFFING AND HENS / Heat the olive oil in a large skillet over medium-high heat, and sauté the onion, coriander seeds, and apricots until the onion begins to soften, about 3 minutes. Transfer the mixture to a large bowl and allow to cool slightly. Add the rice and egg and stir until blended.

Lay each game hen breast-side down on a cutting board. Using kitchen shears, cut through the rib bones on either side of the backbone to free the bone, and remove. Sprinkle the cavity generously with salt and pepper and sprinkle the skin liberally with salt. Pack some of the stuffing into each bird, and tie up with butcher's twine or silicone bands. Lay the hens, breast-side up, in the slow cooker. Cover and cook the hens on low for 7 to 8 hours, basting twice with the sauce during cooking. The hens will be tender and register 170°F/77°C on an instant-read meat thermometer.

Carefully remove the hens from the sauce, transfer to a serving platter, and cut the butcher's twine. Cover with aluminum foil to keep warm. Skim any excess fat from the sauce, transfer the sauce to a saucepan, and bring to a boil. Whisk the cornstarch mixture into the sauce, and continue whisking until the sauce returns to a boil and is smooth and thickened. Taste for seasoning and correct with salt and pepper. Stir in the cilantro. Spoon some of the sauce over the hens and serve, passing the remaining sauce on the side.

Pomegranate-Glazed Turkey Breast with Bread Stuffing

SERVES 8

For years I have been teaching a sell-out do-ahead Thanksgiving class to students all over the country, and many times, students want to cook only a turkey breast for the big day, since their family will eat only white meat. A turkey breast cooked in the slow cooker emerges tender and succulent, never dry or overcooked. This gorgeous, red-glazed turkey breast has a luscious bread stuffing with leeks, dried apple, and smoky ham, which is a delicious complement to the tangy pomegranate-and-apple sauce. Don't wait for Thanksgiving to cook this winner!

TO MAKE THE STUFFING / In a large skillet, melt the butter over medium-high heat, and sauté the leek, dried apples, ham, thyme, and sage until the leek is softened, 2 to 3 minutes. Transfer the mixture to a large mixing bowl, and allow to cool slightly. Add the bread cubes and drizzle in the broth, a bit at a time, to moisten the bread. The mixture should hold together when pinched between your fingers. Season with salt and pepper, and set aside.

TO MAKE THE TURKEY / Pour 2 tbsp of the olive oil into the insert of a 5- to 7-qt/4.5- to 6.5-L slow cooker, add the onion, carrots, and apples and season with salt and pepper. Toss to coat the vegetables.

Season the turkey with salt and pepper. Spread out the stuffing on the turkey breast, leaving about a ½-in/12-mm border on all sides. Roll the turkey around the stuffing, beginning on one side, and tucking in the ends. Tie with butcher's twine or silicone bands at 1-in/2.5-cm intervals. Sprinkle the turkey with salt and pepper.

Heat the remaining 2 tbsp olive oil in a large skillet, over medium-high heat, and brown the turkey on all sides. Transfer to the insert of the slow cooker. Pour the molasses, cider, and broth into the skillet, and bring to a boil, scraping up any browned bits on the bottom of the pan. Pour the liquid over the turkey in the slow cooker. Cover and cook on high for 3 to 4 hours, basting twice during the cooking time with the pan juices. The stuffing in the turkey should register 170°F/71°C on an instant-read meat thermometer.

CONTINUED /

FOR THE STUFFING

2 tbsp unsalted butter

1 leek (white and tender green parts), cleaned and finely chopped

½ cup/85 g dried apples, finely chopped

½ cup/85 g finely diced smoked ham

1 tsp dried thyme

1 tsp dried sage (not rubbed)

4 cups/400 g dried bread cubes, cut into ½-in/12-mm pieces

½ cup/120 ml chicken broth

Salt

Freshly ground black pepper

FOR THE TURKEY

4 tbsp/60 ml extra-virgin olive oil

1 large onion, coarsely chopped

3 medium carrots, coarsely chopped

2 medium Gala apples, peeled, cored, and coarsely chopped

Salt

Freshly ground black pepper

One 4- to 5-lb/1.8- to 2.3-kg turkey breast, preferably boneless (see Slow Cooker Savvy)

¼ cup/60 ml pomegranate molasses

¼ cup/60 ml apple cider

2 cups/480 ml chicken broth or reconstituted demi-glace

2 tbsp cornstarch mixed with 2 tbsp water

Using tongs, carefully remove the turkey from the insert, and transfer to a cutting board. Cover with aluminum foil while making the sauce. Using an immersion blender, purée the sauce and transfer to a saucepan. Bring the sauce to a boil. Whisk in the cornstarch mixture, and continue whisking until the sauce returns to a boil and is smooth and thickened. Remove the twine from the turkey, peel off the skin, and carve into ½-in-/12-mm-thick slices. Serve the turkey in a pool of the sauce.

SLOW COOKER SAVVY

If you prefer to leave the sauce chunky, there is no need to use the immersion blender. The apples and vegetables can be mashed with a potato masher if desired.

In most poultry recipes, I recommend removing the skin before cooking, but for this dish the skin helps to keep the turkey moist in the cooker.

Many full-service grocers will bone the turkey breast for you, but you can also do it yourself: Lay the turkey on a cutting board, skin-side down. Using a flexible boning knife, slice through the cartilage in the center of the breast. Withdraw the knife, and from the skin side, push the center bone (keel bone) toward you. With your knife, push the breast meat away from the center bone, following the curvature of the bone, and remove the bone from the meat. On either side of the breast, slip the knife under the rib bones, and carefully slide the knife toward the center, until you are able to pull the ribs away from the breast. Repeat on the other side. Remove the wishbone if it is still attached, slipping the knife underneath, and scraping the meat from the bone to remove it.

Turkey au Vin

Coq au vin, literally "chicken in wine," is a rustic dish served in bistros across France. Since turkey breast is available in most supermarkets and doesn't tend to dry out in the long cooking process, this is my riff on the classic *coq au vin*. It's traditionally made with a full-bodied French wine such as Burgundy, but you can substitute Merlot or Zinfandel with terrific results. Marinating the turkey in the wine before cooking gives it a deeper flavor. I love to serve this as a party dish; the slow cooker keeps the turkey warm, and the aromas are enticing. Serve this bit of France over buttered noodles or creamy mashed potatoes.

In a mixing bowl, combine the wine, garlic, thyme, bay leaves, salt, and pepper and whisk until blended. Put the turkey in a large zipper-top plastic bag, and add the marinade. Seal the bag and refrigerate for at least 8 hours up to 24 hours.

When ready to proceed, remove the turkey from the marinade and pour the marinade into a saucepan. Boil the marinade for 5 minutes and set aside. In a large skillet, heat the olive oil over medium-high heat and cook the bacon until crisp. Transfer to the insert of a 5- to 7-qt/4.5- to 6.5-L slow cooker. Brown the turkey in the skillet in batches over medium-high heat, taking care not to crowd the pan. Transfer to the insert of the slow cooker. Pour the reserved marinade into the skillet, bring to a boil, and scrape up any browned bits that may be stuck to the bottom of the pan. Pour the marinade into the slow-cooker insert, and add the demi-glace. Cover and cook on high for 3 hours, or on low for 5 to 6 hours, until the turkey is tender.

While the turkey is cooking, wipe out the skillet and melt 2 tbsp of the butter. Sauté the onions until they are browned, 5 to 7 minutes. Add the mushrooms to the pan, season with salt and pepper, and sauté until the onions turn pale gold. Set the mixture aside until the stew is ready. Allow the remaining 2 tbsp butter to soften at room temperature in a small bowl and knead with the flour.

When the turkey is tender, carefully remove it from the sauce with a slotted spoon, and transfer to a bowl. Skim off any excess fat from the sauce, pour the sauce into a saucepan, and bring to a boil. Whisk in the butter mixture, 1 tsp at a time, and continue whisking until the sauce returns to a boil and is smooth and thickened to your liking. Add the onion and mushroom mixture and any accumulated juices to the pan, and stir in the parsley. Return the sauce and turkey to the slow cooker and keep on the warm setting until ready to serve.

4 cups/960 ml full-bodied red wine, such as Burgundy, Merlot, or Zinfandel

2 garlic cloves, minced

1½ tsp dried thyme

2 bay leaves

1½ tsp salt

½ tsp freshly ground black pepper

3 lb/1.4 kg turkey breast, cut into 1-in/2.5-cm pieces

2 tbsp extra-virgin olive oil

8 strips thick-cut bacon, cut into 1-in/2.5-cm pieces

2½ cups/600 ml reconstituted chicken demi-glace, or chicken broth mixed with 2 tbsp soup base

4 tbsp/55 g unsalted butter

¼ lb/113 g cipollini or pearl onions, peeled

1 lb/455 g white button mushrooms, stems trimmed

2 tbsp all-purpose flour

¼ cup/15 g finely chopped fresh flat-leaf parsley

CH.04

SEAFOOD

❧

Harvesting the sea is a way of life for many in the Mediterranean region. Fishermen have plied the local waters for centuries, and fathers continue to teach their sons the necessary skills. Watching the fishermen leave the docks in Genoa, Marseilles, Barcelona, Algiers, Tunis, and Naples, and awaiting their return with the catch of day, is part of the market scene in these and other Mediterranean ports. The catch is a matter of pride for each fisherman, who never would consider selling something that is not the best that he can bring in.

With a slow cooker you can serve up some delectable seafood, mingling the flavors of the Mediterranean, and producing tender and delicious entrées, from a seafood stew prepared with sea bass and North African flavors (see page 123), to halibut baked with potatoes and the flavors of Provence (see page 114), to Olive Oil–Poached Tuna (page 107). Or how about a Spanish paella (see page 116)? Lifting the lid on a seafood dish and inhaling the aroma will make you feel as if you are dining at a seaside bistro along the Mediterranean.

Slow-Cooked Salmon with Sorrel

SERVES 6

Bright pink salmon and deep green sorrel pair up to braise in a lemony, white wine–butter sauce. Once the salmon is cooked, the sauce is puréed with a bit of cream and served over the salmon; it doesn't get much easier than that! If you can't find sorrel, substitute watercress or leeks.

Pour the butter into the insert of a 5- to 7-qt/4.5- to 6.5-L slow cooker, and stir in the lemon juice and white wine. Toss the sorrel with the wine mixture, and set aside.

In a small bowl, mix together the olive oil and Old Bay. Use a brush to paint the mixture over the salmon, and lay the salmon on top of the sorrel in the slow cooker. Cover and cook on high for 1½ to 2 hours, or on low for 3 to 4 hours, until the salmon is opaque in the center and registers 165°F/74°C on an instant-read meat thermometer.

Carefully remove the salmon from the slow cooker with a long fish spatula, set it on a cutting board, and cover with aluminum foil while making the sauce.

Using an immersion blender, purée the sauce in the slow cooker, or allow it to cool slightly and purée in a blender. Transfer the sauce to a small saucepan over medium-high heat. Stir in the cream, season with salt and pepper, and bring the sauce to a simmer. Remove from the heat. If the salmon had skin on it, remove it before serving; it should slip right off. Serve the salmon in a pool of sorrel sauce, and pass any additional sauce on the side.

4 tbsp/55 g unsalted butter, melted

2 tbsp fresh lemon juice

1 cup/240 ml dry white wine, such as Pinot Grigio or Sauvignon Blanc, or dry vermouth

1 cup/100 g packed sorrel, tough stems removed, and finely chopped

2 tbsp extra-virgin olive oil

1 tsp Old Bay Seasoning or seafood seasoning

One 2½- to 3-lb/1.2- to 1.4-kg side of salmon

½ cup/120 ml heavy cream

Salt

Freshly ground black pepper

Smothered Tuna Siciliana

¼ cup/60 ml extra-virgin olive oil

3 garlic cloves, sliced

1 medium onion, finely chopped

1 tsp dried oregano

Pinch of red pepper flakes (optional)

1 cup/240 ml dry white wine, such as Pinot Grigio or Sauvignon Blanc, or dry vermouth

One 28- to 32-oz/800- to 910-g can chopped tomatoes, with their juice

½ cup/50 g capers packed in brine, drained and large ones chopped

½ cup/50 g pitted oil-cured olives

Grated zest of 1 lemon

4 lb/1.8 kg tuna steaks, about 1 in/2.5 cm thick

Salt

Freshly ground black pepper

½ cup/30 g finely chopped fresh flat-leaf parsley

An Italian fisherman once told me that tuna should either be cooked quickly, or long and slow. This recipe falls into the long and slow category, and it suits the slow cooker perfectly. The tuna simmers in a sauce with tomato, capers, olives, and lemon, resulting in fork-tender fish and a zesty sauce to serve over orzo or rice. I've used oregano in this recipe, but you can substitute thyme, sage, or rosemary if you prefer.

In a large skillet, heat the olive oil over medium-high heat and sauté the garlic, onion, oregano, and red pepper flakes (if using) for 3 minutes, or until the onion begins to soften. Add the white wine and bring to a boil. Transfer the contents of the skillet to the insert of a 5- to 7-qt/4.5- to 6.5-L slow cooker. Stir in the tomatoes, capers, olives, and lemon zest. Push the tuna under the sauce. Cover the slow cooker and cook on low for 5 to 6 hours, until the tuna is fork-tender. (Do not cook the tuna on high; it will be tough and chewy.)

Carefully remove the tuna from the slow cooker with a large spatula, transfer to a serving dish, and cover with aluminum foil. Skim off any excess fat from the sauce, season with salt and pepper, and stir in the parsley. Serve the tuna napped with some of the sauce, and pass the extra sauce on the side.

SLOW COOKER SAVVY

Most tuna steaks will come with the skin on. Wait until after the tuna is cooked to remove the skin; it will peel right off.

If you have tuna and sauce left over, chunk the tuna into the sauce and serve it over pasta.

Olive Oil–Poached Tuna

SERVES 6

Mediterranean cooks have been preserving tuna and other fish in olive oil for centuries, much like the French preserve duck confit. The tuna poaches in the oil, becoming soft and flavorful. Serve it immediately as a main course, or refrigerate and use in salads and pasta sauces. Be sure to use a high-quality extra-virgin olive oil here; it makes a huge difference in the quality of the finished dish.

5 to 6 cups/1.2 to 1.4 L extra-virgin olive oil

6 garlic cloves, sliced

Pinch of red pepper flakes

3 lb/1.4 kg tuna steaks, about 1 in/2.5 cm thick

Pour 5 cups/1.2 L of the olive oil into the insert of a 5- to 7-qt/4.5- to 6.5-L slow cooker and stir in the garlic and red pepper flakes. Submerge the tuna in the oil. (If you need more oil to completely cover the tuna, add it now.) Cover the slow cooker and cook on low for 3 to 4 hours, until the tuna is cooked through.

Carefully lift the tuna out of the slow cooker with a wide fish spatula, and transfer to a cutting board. Remove any skin on the tuna, and cool. To preserve the tuna in the refrigerator, strain the oil and store the tuna in the oil in a closed container for up to 2 months. Or drain the tuna and refrigerate, tightly wrapped, for up to 1 week.

Swordfish Piccata

3 lb/1.4 kg swordfish fillets

2 tbsp extra-virgin olive oil

½ cup/80 g finely chopped onion

4 garlic cloves, minced

Pinch of red pepper flakes

Grated zest of 1 lemon

1 tsp dried Greek or Italian oregano

One 14½- to 15-oz/415- to 430-g can chopped tomatoes, with their juice

½ cup/50 g capers packed in brine, drained and chopped if large

¼ cup/15 g finely chopped fresh flat-leaf parsley

Salt

Freshly ground black pepper

Cooked angel hair pasta, for serving (optional)

The word *piccata* is not found in Italian-English dictionaries. Some people think it is the term for a veal scallop, but others believe it is a shortened version of the word *piccante*, meaning "spicy" or "hot." This dish features all the salty, spicy good-ness that the Mediterranean has to offer in a great seafood main course. It's terrific with any fish with firm, dense flesh. If you like, serve it over angel hair pasta.

Put the swordfish into the insert of a 5- to 7-qt/4.5- to 6.5-L slow cooker. In a large skillet, heat the olive oil over medium-high heat, and sauté the onion, garlic, red pepper flakes, lemon zest, and oregano for 3 minutes, or until the onion begins to soften. Add the tomatoes, and stir to blend. Transfer the contents of the skillet to the insert, stir in the capers, and submerge the fish. Cover and cook on high for 1 hour, or on low for 2½ to 3 hours.

Stir the parsley into the sauce and season with salt and pepper. Using a fish spatula, transfer the fish to a serving platter, and top with the sauce. Or serve the fish over angel hair pasta, with some of the sauce on the side.

Braised Swordfish
in the Style of the Greek Isles

SERVES 6

¼ cup/60 ml extra-virgin olive oil

2 garlic cloves, minced

2 tsp dried Greek oregano

1 tsp sweet paprika

½ cup/120 ml fresh lemon juice

1 cup/240 ml dry white wine, such as Pinot Grigio or Sauvignon Blanc, or dry vermouth

2½ lb/1.2 kg swordfish fillets

½ cup/30 g finely chopped fresh flat-leaf parsley

1 lemon, thinly sliced

When I think of Greek fish dishes, I think of lemon, garlic, oregano, and lots of great extra-virgin olive oil to flavor the fish. This dish has all of that. Swordfish has a bold flavor; if you would like to substitute another fish, choose one with dense flesh, like halibut, snapper, sea bass, cod, or salmon.

In a small skillet, heat the olive oil over medium heat and sauté the garlic, oregano, and paprika for 2 minutes, until the garlic is fragrant. Transfer the mixture to the insert of a 5- to 7-qt/4.5- to 6.5-L slow cooker. Stir in the lemon juice and wine. Arrange the swordfish in the bottom of the slow cooker, spooning the sauce over the fish. Cover the slow cooker and cook on high for 1 hour, or on low for 2 hours.

Using a spatula, transfer the swordfish to a serving platter, and remove any skin or bones. Add the parsley to the sauce, and spoon it over the fish. Garnish the fish with the lemon slices and serve.

VARIATION If you would like to add a vegetable to the fish, baby artichokes are a great choice. Cut off the stems and snap off the tough outer leaves of 6 baby artichokes. Quarter the artichokes and add them to the liquid in the slow cooker; the cooking time will remain the same.

Monkfish Braised with Peppers

Monkfish is a rather ugly fish, but it is rich and delicious, especially when braised in white wine with confetti-colored bell peppers. This dish is terrific served over rice or pasta. If you can't get monkfish, substitute cod, halibut, or sea bass.

In a large skillet, heat the olive oil over medium-high heat, and sauté the onion, thyme, and bell peppers for 5 to 7 minutes, or until the onion is softened. Add the wine and tomato purée, and stir to combine. Transfer the mixture to the insert of a 5- to 7-qt/4.5- to 6.5-L slow cooker. Lay the monkfish on top of the bell peppers, spooning some of the sauce over the top. Cover and cook on high for 1½ hours, or on low for 3 hours, until the fish is cooked through.

Carefully remove the monkfish from the slow cooker with a large spatula and transfer to a platter. Serve topped with the sauce.

2 tbsp extra-virgin olive oil

1 large sweet yellow onion, such as Vidalia, thinly sliced

1 tsp dried thyme

1 medium yellow bell pepper, cored and thinly sliced

1 medium orange bell pepper, cored and thinly sliced

1 medium red bell pepper, cored and thinly sliced

1 cup/240 ml dry white wine, such as Pinot Grigio or Sauvignon Blanc, or dry vermouth

½ cup/120 ml tomato purée

2½ lb/1.1 kg monkfish fillets

Salt Cod and Potatoes

1 lb/455 g salt cod

4 cups/960 ml milk

¼ cup/60 ml extra-virgin olive oil

1 medium onion, finely chopped

Pinch of red pepper flakes

2 garlic cloves, minced

1 tsp dried oregano

1 cup/240 ml dry white wine, such as Pinot Grigio or Sauvignon Blanc, or dry vermouth

One 28- to 32-oz/800- to 910-g can chopped tomatoes, with their juice

1 lb/455 g tiny new potatoes (red, white, or Yukon gold), scrubbed, and skin left on if perfect

¼ cup/15 g finely chopped fresh flat-leaf parsley

Salt

Freshly ground black pepper

Salt cod is popular along the northern Mediterranean, and it appears in many traditional dishes, such as Sicilian fritters and a Provençal purée called *brandade*. This important dietary staple makes a great slow-cooked one-pot meal. My *nonna* would make this dish on cold wintry days, and the smell was so enticing, even to a child who wasn't fond of the smell of the *baccalà* in the Italian grocery store. Serve it with sautéed Swiss chard, escarole, or spinach. Salt cod needs to be soaked 2 days ahead of time to remove the salt and make it easy for you to remove the bones and skin before cooking.

Break the cod into pieces that will fit into a 9-by-13-in/23-by-33-cm baking dish. Put the cod in the dish, cover with the milk, and turn over the fish. Cover and refrigerate for 2 days, turning the cod to make sure that it is soaking in the milk. When the cod has soaked, drain it and discard the milk. Remove any bones and skin from the cod, wash it under cold running water, and set aside.

In a large skillet, heat the olive oil over medium-high heat and sauté the onion, red pepper flakes, garlic, and oregano for 3 minutes, or until the onion begins to soften. Add the wine, bring to a boil, and let it evaporate a bit. Transfer the contents of the skillet to the insert of a 4- to 6-qt/3.5- to 5.5-L slow cooker, and stir in the tomatoes. Add the cod, pushing it down into the sauce, and arrange the potatoes in the insert. Cover and cook on high for 3 hours, or on low for 6 hours, until the potatoes are tender.

Stir in the parsley, season with salt and pepper, and serve.

Pesto-Glazed Cod
on a Bed of Risotto

Although this dish is made with cod, any fish with thick flesh, such as snapper, halibut, or sea bass, will work here. A fragrant basil and sun-dried tomato pesto gives this simple fish a lovely flavor, and the bed of creamy rice beneath the cod is infused with the flavors of the fish and the pesto. Basil pesto is a classic sauce from the seaport of Genoa. The addition here of sun-dried tomatoes and a bit of balsamic vinegar gives it a lot of personality.

TO MAKE THE PESTO / In a food processor, combine the tomatoes, garlic, basil, pine nuts, and Parmigiano-Reggiano and process for about 1 minute. With the machine running, gradually add the olive oil and vinegar and process until thoroughly incorporated. Scrape down the sides of the bowl and process for another 30 seconds. Taste and season with salt and pepper.

Spread a ¼-in/6-mm layer of the pesto over the cod fillets, and refrigerate until ready to cook.

TO MAKE THE RICE / In a large skillet, melt 4 tbsp of the butter over medium-high heat, add the onion, and sauté for 3 minutes, until softened. Add the rice and cook for another 1 minute to coat the rice grains. Add the wine and bring to a boil. Transfer the mixture to the insert of a 5- to 7-qt/4.5- to 6.5-L slow cooker, and stir in the stock.

Carefully place the pesto-coated cod over the rice. Cover the slow cooker and cook on high for 1 hour, until the rice is creamy and the fish is opaque.

Carefully lift the cod out of the slow cooker using a fish spatula, and transfer to a plate. Stir the remaining 2 tbsp butter into the rice, and transfer the rice to a serving platter. Arrange the fish over the rice, and garnish with the chopped basil before serving.

FOR THE PESTO

1½ cups/150 g oil-packed sun-dried tomatoes

6 garlic cloves, peeled

1 cup/45 g packed fresh basil leaves

½ cup/55 g pine nuts

1 cup/115 g freshly grated Parmigiano-Reggiano cheese

½ cup/120 ml olive oil

2 tbsp balsamic vinegar

Salt

Freshly ground black pepper

2½ to 3 lb/1.2 to 1.4 kg Atlantic cod fillets

FOR THE RICE

6 tbsp/85 g unsalted butter

½ cup/80 g finely chopped sweet yellow onion, such as Vidalia

2 cups/430 g Arborio rice

½ cup/120 ml dry white wine, such as Pinot Grigio or Sauvignon Blanc, or dry vermouth

4 cups/960 ml seafood stock, or 2 cups clam juice mixed with 2 cups chicken broth

¼ cup/10 g packed basil leaves, finely chopped, for garnish

Halibut Provençal

½ cup/120 ml extra-virgin olive oil

Grated zest of 2 lemons

¼ cup/60 ml fresh lemon juice

4 garlic cloves, minced

1½ tsp salt

½ tsp freshly ground black pepper

½ tsp sweet paprika

2 tsp herbes de Provence (see Slow Cooker Savvy)

½ cup/50 g oil-packed sun-dried tomatoes, drained

½ cup/50 g capers packed in brine, drained and chopped if large

1 lb/455 g small Yukon gold potatoes, quartered

Six 6-oz/170-g halibut fillets or other thick-fleshed fish

½ cup/30 g finely chopped fresh flat-leaf parsley, for garnish

The sunny flavors of Provence, in the South of France, infuse this lovely seafood dish. A layer of Yukon gold potatoes soaks up the flavor of thick-cut halibut fillets covered with a lemon, garlic, and caper sauce. If you are unable to get halibut, any fish with dense flesh will work here, so try salmon, sea bass, or cod.

In a mixing bowl, whisk together the olive oil, lemon zest and juice, garlic, salt, pepper, paprika, herbes de Provence, sun-dried tomatoes, and capers and set aside.

Coat the insert of a 4- to 6-qt/3.5- to 5.5-L slow cooker with nonstick cooking spray, or line it with a slow-cooker liner. Arrange the potatoes in the slow cooker. Drizzle some of the lemon sauce mixture over the potatoes, and toss to coat the potatoes. Arrange the halibut over the potatoes, and pour the remaining sauce over the halibut. Cover the slow cooker and cook on high for 2 hours, or on low for 3½ to 4 hours. The fish will be opaque in the center and the potatoes will be tender.

Arrange the fish on a serving platter, surround with the potatoes, and spoon some of the sauce over the fish. Garnish with chopped parsley before serving.

SLOW COOKER SAVVY

Herbes de Provence is an herb blend from the Southern region of France, generally a mixture of dried basil, sage, rosemary, marjoram, thyme, savory, and fennel. Some French cooks also include lavender in the mix.

Shrimp with White Beans, Sun-Dried Tomatoes, and Basil

Creamy white beans become flavorful and tinted pink when cooked with sun-dried tomatoes. In the last hour of cooking, plump, succulent shrimp are added to the pot to simmer, giving the beans a briny finish. Don't forget to soak the beans the night before you want to make this dish.

In a colander, wash the beans in cold water, picking them over for any broken beans or stones. Put the beans in a large bowl, and cover with at least 2 in/5 cm of cold water. Cover with plastic wrap, and let soak overnight. Rinse the beans thoroughly, and put them in the insert of a 5- to 7-qt/4.5- to 6.5-L slow cooker.

In a large skillet, heat 2 tbsp of the olive oil over medium-high heat and sauté the garlic, onion, and sun-dried tomatoes for 3 minutes, or until the onion begins to soften. Spoon some of the broth into the skillet, and transfer the contents of the skillet to the insert. Stir the rest of the broth into the bean mixture. Cover and cook on low for 7 hours.

Add the shrimp, pushing them underneath the beans. Cover and cook on low for another 45 minutes to 1 hour, until the shrimp are pink and cooked through.

Stir the basil and remaining 2 tbsp of olive oil into the beans, season with salt and pepper, and serve.

2 cups/440 g small dried white beans

4 tbsp/60 ml extra-virgin olive oil

4 garlic cloves, minced

½ cup/80 g finely chopped onion

½ cup/50 g oil-packed sun-dried tomatoes, drained and finely chopped

6 to 7 cups/1.4 to 1.7 L chicken broth

1 lb/455 g large shrimp, peeled, deveined, and tails removed

¼ cup/10 g packed fresh basil leaves, finely chopped

Salt

Freshly ground black pepper

Paella Valenciana

2 tbsp olive oil

1½ lb/675 g Spanish (not Mexican) chorizo sausage, cut into ½-in-/12-mm-thick rounds

4 boneless, skinless chicken breast halves, cut into bite-size pieces

1 cup/160 g finely chopped red onion

4 garlic cloves, cut into slivers

1 large red bell pepper, cored and cut into ½-in-/12-mm-wide strips

1 large yellow bell pepper, cored and cut into ½-in-/12-mm-wide strips

Two 14½- to 15-oz/415- to 430-g cans chopped tomatoes, with their juice

1 tsp saffron threads, crushed in the palm of your hand

½ tsp freshly ground black pepper

8 to 10 cups/2 to 2.4 L chicken broth

3 cups/645 g Arborio rice

1½ lb/680 g jumbo shrimp, peeled, deveined, and tails removed

24 littleneck or cherrystone clams, scrubbed

2 cups/200 g shelled fresh peas or frozen petite peas, defrosted

4 lemons, cut into wedges, for garnish

1 cup/60 g chopped fresh flat-leaf parsley, for garnish

A party in a pot is how I would define this dish. Paella is the national dish of Spain; it originated in Valencia, where it was first made in the fields over an open fire. Saffron, short-grain rice, and Spanish chorizo are traditionally found in paella. The other ingredients depend on the region and the chef. This paella is filled with chicken and seafood. Bursting with flavor, it's ready in about 2 hours.

Heat the olive oil in a large skillet over medium-high heat, add the sausage and render some of the fat. Transfer the sausage to the insert of a 5- to 7-qt/4.5- to 6.5-L slow cooker. Brown the chicken in the skillet, and transfer to the slow cooker insert. Add the onion, garlic, and bell peppers to the skillet and cook, stirring, until they begin to soften, about 3 minutes. Stir in the tomatoes, saffron, and pepper, and bring to a boil, scraping up any browned bits on the bottom of the pan. Transfer the mixture to the slow-cooker insert and add the broth. Cover and cook on high for 1 hour, or on low for 2 hours.

Add the rice, shrimp, clams, and peas, pushing down on the clams so they are underneath the rice. Cover and cook for another hour on high, or 2 hours on low, until the shrimp are pink and the rice is tender.

Discard any clams that haven't opened. Transfer the paella to a platter and serve, garnished with lemon wedges and chopped parsley.

Moroccan Seafood Stew

Sea bass is bathed in a tomato sauce fragrant with saffron, orange, and garlic; a bit of hot paprika gives it some kick. This seafood stew makes a great main course any time of the year and is delicious with couscous or rice on the side. The sea bass is my first choice because it's almost impossible to overcook thanks to its protein structure. If sea bass isn't available, try halibut, snapper, or cod.

In a large skillet, heat the olive oil over medium-high heat, and sauté the onion, bell peppers, garlic, saffron, sweet paprika, hot paprika (if using) and ginger for 3 minutes, or until the onion begins to soften. Add the tomatoes and sauté for another 2 minutes, to blend the flavors. Transfer the mixture to the insert of a 5- to 7-qt/4.5- to 6.5-L slow cooker and stir in the orange juice. Place the sea bass on top of the tomato mixture, and spoon some of the mixture over the fish. Cover and cook for 2 hours on high, or 3 to 4 hours on low. At the end of the cooking time, the sea bass should be opaque in the center.

Using a fish spatula, carefully lift the fish out of the slow cooker, transfer to a serving platter, and cover loosely with aluminum foil. Skim off any excess fat from the sauce, stir in the parsley and cilantro, and season with salt and pepper. Spoon some of the sauce over the fish, and garnish the platter with the orange slices. Serve immediately, passing the remaining sauce on the side.

2 tbsp extra-virgin olive oil

1 large onion, finely chopped

1 medium red bell pepper, cored and cut into ½-in/12-mm strips

1 medium yellow bell pepper, cored and cut into ½-in/12-mm strips

4 garlic cloves, minced

1 tsp saffron threads, crushed in the palm of your hand

1½ tsp sweet paprika

¼ tsp hot paprika (optional, but oh so good)

½ tsp ground ginger

One 14½- to 15-oz/415- to 430-g can chopped tomatoes, with their juice

¼ cup/60 ml fresh orange juice

2 lb/910 g sea bass fillets

¼ cup/15 g finely chopped fresh flat-leaf parsley

¼ cup/15 g finely chopped fresh cilantro

Salt

Freshly ground black pepper

1 navel orange, thinly sliced, for garnish

Bouillabaisse

3 tbsp extra-virgin olive oil

2 leeks (white and tender green parts), cleaned and thinly sliced

3 garlic cloves, minced

1 fennel bulb, wispy fronds removed, finely diced

2 tsp grated orange zest

1 tsp saffron threads, crushed in the palm of your hand

1 cup/240 ml dry white wine, such as Pinot Grigio or Sauvignon Blanc, or dry vermouth

¼ cup/60 ml tomato paste

6 cups/1.4 L seafood stock, or 3 cups/720 ml clam juice and 3 cups/720 ml chicken broth

1½ lb/680 g sea bass fillet

1½ lb/680 g mussels, scrubbed and debearded

1 lb/455 g large shrimp, peeled, deveined, and tails removed

½ cup/30 g finely chopped fresh flat-leaf parsley

Salt

Freshly ground black pepper

Rouille (facing page), for serving

8 slices French bread, toasted, for serving

This saffron-and-fennel-scented fish stew originated near Marseilles, in Provence. No one is quite sure how it came to be, but the addition of saffron leads me to believe that it may have been an import from Spain or Morocco. Bouillabaisse is traditionally served with toasted bread slices spread with a garlicky saffron-flavored mayonnaise called a rouille. It can be addictive all by itself, and it adds a lot of flavor to the stew, when allowed to mingle with the broth.

Heat the olive oil in a large skillet over medium-high heat, and sauté the leeks, garlic, fennel, orange zest, and saffron for 2 to 3 minutes, until the leeks are softened. Add the wine and tomato paste and bring to a boil, scraping up any browned bits on the bottom of the pan. Transfer the mixture to the insert of a 5- to 7-qt/ 4.5- to 6.5-L slow cooker and stir in the stock. Cover and cook on high for 2 hours, or on low for 4 hours.

Add the sea bass and mussels, cover, and cook for another 30 minutes on high, or 1 hour on low.

Add the shrimp and cook for another 20 minutes on high, or 40 minutes on low. Check to make sure that all the mussels have opened; if any are still closed, discard them. Stir in the parsley and season with salt and pepper.

Serve the bouillabaisse in large shallow bowls. Spread some of the rouille over each slice of toasted bread, and float a slice on each serving of bouillabaisse.

Rouille

MAKES ABOUT 1½ CUPS

With all the concern over making your own mayonnaise with raw eggs, I've eliminated that problem by using prepared mayonnaise for a simpler and safer treat. It will keep in the refrigerator for up to 1 week.

1 tsp saffron threads, crushed in the palm of your hand

2 tbsp fresh lemon juice

4 garlic cloves, minced

Pinch of red pepper flakes

1¼ cups/300 ml mayonnaise

Salt

Freshly ground black pepper

In a medium bowl, sprinkle the saffron over the lemon juice, and allow to steep for 5 minutes. Whisk in the garlic, red pepper flakes, and mayonnaise, stirring until blended. Season with salt and pepper. Cover and refrigerate for at least 2 hours, or up to 1 week.

PASTA, RICE, AND OTHER GRAINS

Throughout the Mediterranean, pasta, rice, and other grains are eaten daily. They are the backbone of the region's cuisines, helping to absorb savory sauces, and enriching many dishes with their starchy goodness. Rice and legumes are staples that appear on countless Mediterranean tables. Pasta and polenta have rich traditions in Italy, while couscous—tiny granules made from semolina flour—is popular in the North African and Middle Eastern regions of the Mediterranean.

When I began to test recipes, I had no idea that polenta—a marathon affair on the stove top involving endless stirring to get the right consistency—could be made in the slow cooker, with just a few whisks in the cooker and an hour on high. The result is as creamy and satisfying as the classic version.

Risotto, that creamy rice dish from Milan, which also involves a lot of stirring, is made just as easily in the slow cooker as polenta. The cooker also provides a low and slow oven for some of your favorite layered pasta dishes, such as lasagna and Greek pastitsio. The result is tender pasta with intense flavors that develop over the long, lazy cooking time. So come along for an adventure in slow cooking, where you will make Pilaf (page 141), risotto (see pages 139 and 140), lasagna (see pages 130, 131, and 132), Polenta (page 137), and more, all with a little work and a lot of flavor!

Pastitsio

FOR THE MEAT SAUCE

1 tbsp extra-virgin olive oil

1 lb/455 g lean ground beef

½ lb/225 g ground lamb

1 medium onion, finely chopped

1 tsp salt

¼ tsp freshly ground black pepper

⅛ tsp freshly grated nutmeg

⅛ tsp ground cinnamon

2 cups/480 ml tomato purée

1 cup/115 g freshly grated kefalotyri or Asiago cheese

FOR THE CREAM SAUCE

2 tbsp unsalted butter

2 tbsp all-purpose flour

2 cups/480 ml whole milk

1 tsp salt

½ tsp freshly ground black pepper

4 large eggs, beaten

1 cup/115 g freshly grated kefalotyri, Asiago, or Parmigiano-Reggiano cheese

1 lb/455 g elbow macaroni

3 tbsp unsalted butter, melted

1¼ cups/145 g freshly grated Parmigiano-Reggiano cheese

½ tsp sweet paprika

This delicious macaroni and meat dish is served on Greek holidays and for special occasions, but pastitsio is also a terrific party dish. The slow cooker melds all the luscious flavors together, melting the cheeses into the meats and macaroni. The result is a dish fit for the gods. All the components can be made ahead of time, and then layered into the slow cooker so you can set it and forget it. This is terrific as a main course, but it's also a great side dish to serve with roasted lamb or chicken and a huge mixed green salad tossed with red wine vinaigrette, Greek olives, and feta cheese.

TO MAKE THE MEAT SAUCE / In a large saucepan, heat the olive oil over medium-high heat. Brown the beef and lamb, breaking it up as it cooks, until it is no longer pink. Drain off any excess fat or water. Add the onion, salt, pepper, nutmeg, and cinnamon and cook, stirring, until the onion is translucent, another 4 minutes. Add the tomato purée, reduce the heat to medium, and simmer until the juices are absorbed and the sauce is thick, about 20 minutes. Stir in the cheese. (At this point, the meat sauce can be cooled, covered, and refrigerated for up to 2 days.)

TO MAKE THE CREAM SAUCE / In a medium saucepan, melt the butter over medium heat. When the foam subsides, add the flour and cook, whisking constantly. When white bubbles form on the surface, cook for 2 to 3 minutes more, still whisking. Slowly add the milk, whisking until the sauce is smooth and comes to boil. Add the salt and pepper, remove from the heat, and whisk in the eggs and cheese, stirring until the cheese is melted. (At this point, the cream sauce can be cooled, covered, and refrigerated for up to 2 days.)

Before you assemble the dish, cook the macaroni in a large pot of salted water for 3 minutes short of al dente and drain. Stir the melted butter into the hot macaroni, and then add 1 cup/115 g of the Parmigiano, stirring until it is almost melted.

Coat the inside of a 4- to 6-qt/3.5- to 5.5-L slow cooker with nonstick cooking spray, or line it with a slow-cooker liner. Layer half of the cheesy macaroni in the bottom. Spread a third of the cream sauce over the macaroni, and spread all the meat sauce over the cream sauce. Cover the meat sauce with half the remaining cream sauce. Layer the remaining macaroni on top, and spread with the remaining cream sauce. Sprinkle the top evenly with the remaining cheese and the paprika. Cover the slow cooker and cook on low for 4 hours, or high for 2 hours.

Uncover the slow cooker and cook for another 30 minutes. Allow the pastitsio to rest for 10 minutes before serving.

Lasagna Bolognese

4 tbsp/55 g unsalted butter

¼ cup/30 g all-purpose flour

1½ cups/360 ml chicken broth

1½ cups/360 ml milk

2½ cups/250 g freshly grated Parmigiano-Reggiano cheese

6 cups/1.4 L Bolognese Sauce (page 75)

One 9-oz/255-g package no-cook lasagna noodles, preferably Barilla

1 lb/455 g fresh mozzarella cheese, cut into ½-in/12-mm slices

A classic recipe from the region of Emilia-Romagna, this lasagna is layered with a Bolognese sauce and a creamy béchamel flavored with Parmigiano-Reggiano, the king of cheeses in this region. I love making lasagna in the slow cooker; the noodles become tender, and infused with the flavors of the sauce over the long, slow cooking time.

Coat the inside of a 5- to 7-qt/4.5- to 6.5-L slow cooker with nonstick cooking spray, or line the cooker with a slow-cooker liner. In a medium saucepan, over medium-high heat, melt the butter. When the foam subsides, add the flour and cook, whisking constantly. When white bubbles begin to form, cook the roux, still whisking, for 2 to 3 minutes. Slowly add the broth and milk, whisking until the mixture comes to a boil. Remove from the heat, and stir in 1½ cups/175 g of the Parmigiano.

Spoon some of the Bolognese sauce on the bottom of the prepared slow cooker. Top with a layer of noodles; depending on the type of machine, you may have to snap the noodles so they fit. Spread a layer of the cream sauce over the noodles, and top with some of the mozzarella. Repeat the layers two or three more times, ending with Bolognese sauce. Sprinkle the top with the remaining Parmigiano. Cover and cook on low for 4 to 5 hours, until the lasagna is bubbling.

Uncover the slow cooker and cook an additional 45 minutes. Serve on the warm setting.

Seafood Lasagna

A terrific party dish, this sumptuous lasagna is filled with shellfish, a creamy sauce, and a bit of marinara to give it some gusto. It is sure to elicit swoons from your guests. The combination of seafood is up to you. Mix the shellfish as I have done here, or use a combination of halibut and shrimp or crab, or all halibut or all sea bass.

TO MAKE THE SEAFOOD / In a large skillet, melt the butter over medium-high heat, add the scallops, shrimp, crabmeat, and wine and cook until the shrimp have turned pink. Transfer the seafood to a colander, strain the cooking liquid, and set aside ⅔ cup/165 ml for the cream sauce. Discard the rest.

TO MAKE THE CREAM SAUCE / In a large saucepan, melt the butter over medium-high heat. When the foam subsides, whisk in the flour and cook, whisking constantly. When bubbles form around the pan, cook for another 2 to 3 minutes, still whisking. Gradually add the milk and reserved seafood cooking liquid, whisking constantly until the sauce comes to a boil. Add the cream and simmer, stirring a few times, until the sauce is thick enough to coat the back of a spoon. Season with salt and add the Tabasco and nutmeg.

Coat the inside of a 5- to 7-qt/4.5- to 6.5-L slow-cooker insert with nonstick cooking spray, or line the insert with a slow-cooker liner. Spread half of the marinara on the bottom of the insert, and top with about a quarter of the lasagna noodles, cutting them to fit the shape of your slow cooker. Top the noodles with half of the seafood mixture, and spoon a third of the cream sauce over the seafood. Cover the seafood with a third of the remaining noodles, and spread the remaining seafood over the noodles. Top with half of the remaining cream sauce, and sprinkle with ½ cup/60 g of the Parmigiano. Cover the seafood with half of the remaining noodles, all of the remaining marinara sauce, and ¼ cup/30 g Parmigiano. Add the remaining noodles in one layer, cover with the remaining cream sauce, and sprinkle evenly with the remaining Parmigiano. Cover and cook on low for 4 to 5 hours, until the noodles are tender and the cheese is bubbling.

Allow the lasagna to rest for 15 minutes, uncovered, before serving.

FOR THE SEAFOOD

4 tbsp/55 g unsalted butter

1 lb/455 g bay scallops, left whole, or sea scallops, quartered

½ lb/225 g medium shrimp, peeled, deveined, and tails removed

½ lb/225 g lump crabmeat, picked over for shells and cartilage

2 tbsp dry white wine, such as Pinot Grigio or Sauvignon Blanc, or dry vermouth

FOR THE CREAM SAUCE

½ cup/115 g unsalted butter

½ cup/65 g all-purpose flour

3 cups/720 ml whole milk

¾ cup/180 ml heavy cream

Salt

4 drops Tabasco

Dash of freshly grated nutmeg

4 cups/960 ml Basic Marinara Sauce (page 176)

One 9-oz/255-g package no-cook lasagna noodles, preferably Barilla

1¼ cups/145 g freshly grated Parmigiano-Reggiano cheese

Wild Mushroom and Truffle Lasagna

SERVES 8

¾ cup/170 g unsalted butter

1 lb/455 g white button or cremini mushrooms (see Slow Cooker Savvy), stems removed and sliced ¼ in/6 mm thick

4 fresh sage leaves, thinly sliced

Salt

Freshly ground black pepper

½ cup/60 g all-purpose flour

3 cups/720 ml chicken broth

2½ cups/600 ml whole milk

1 tsp freshly ground white pepper (black pepper is fine, too)

½ tsp freshly grated nutmeg

2½ cups/290 g freshly grated pecorino romano cheese

One 9-oz/255-g package no-cook lasagna noodles, preferably Barilla (see Slow Cooker Savvy)

¼ lb/115 g thinly sliced prosciutto, cut into narrow strips

1 lb/455 g fresh mozzarella cheese, cut into ½-in/12-mm slices

⅓ cup/75 ml truffle oil, for serving

La Taverna del Lupo ("the Tavern of the Wolf"), in Gubbio, the small Umbrian hill town where my *nonna* was born, serves an incredible white lasagna. It's filled with wafer-thin pasta, sautéed mushrooms, and prosciutto, and it's topped with shaved black truffles and drizzled with truffle oil—heaven on a plate. Like any layered pasta dish, it takes a few steps to get it into the slow cooker, but once it's there, you can feel free to go about your business without worrying that the lasagna will dry out, as it might in the oven. I recommend that you use a slow-cooker liner or nonstick cooking spray with any of the layered pastas. The cheese tends to stick to the insert, and the liner or spray saves you from a laborious cleanup. You can get truffle oil at D'Artagnan (see Resources, page 184).

In a large sauté pan, melt ¼ cup/55 g of the butter over medium-high heat, add the mushrooms and sage, and sauté until the liquid begins to evaporate and the mushrooms begin to color. Season the mushrooms with salt and pepper, remove from the pan, and set aside to cool.

In a medium saucepan, melt the remaining ½ cup/115 g butter over medium-high heat. When the foam subsides, whisk in the flour and cook, whisking constantly. After white bubbles form on the surface, cook for 2 to 3 minutes more, still whisking. Gradually add the broth, whisking until blended. Add the milk, 1½ tsp salt, the white pepper, and nutmeg and bring the mixture to a boil, whisking constantly. Remove the sauce from the heat and gradually add 1½ cups of the pecorino, stirring until it melts. Taste the sauce for seasoning and add more salt and pepper if necessary.

Coat the inside of a 5- to 7-qt/4.5- to 6.5-L slow-cooker insert with nonstick cooking spray, or line with a slow-cooker liner. Spread a layer of cheese sauce in the bottom of the insert, and top with lasagna noodles, breaking them to fit into layers. (If you have an oval slow cooker, adjust the noodles to fit your pan.) Spread some of the mushrooms and prosciutto over the noodles, and top with a bit of the sauce and some of the mozzarella. Repeat the layers a couple of times, ending with the noodles and the remaining cheese sauce. Depending on the type of slow cooker you have, you should have four layers of noodles. Sprinkle the lasagna with the remaining pecorino and any remaining mozzarella. Cover the slow cooker and cook on low for 4 to 5 hours, until the noodles are tender and the cheese on the top has melted.

Uncover the slow cooker and allow the lasagna to rest for 15 minutes before serving. Drizzle each serving with a bit of truffle oil.

SLOW COOKER SAVVY

I've tested hundreds of lasagna noodles, no-boil and boil, and the Barilla brand is superior. The noodles are thin and supple, and the finished dish comes out perfectly every time.

I do not recommend that you make this recipe in an inexpensive slow cooker. They tend to cook very hot and actually can burn the cheese sauce.

Using white buttons and creminis will give you a creamy colored lasagna; if you would like to use other wild mushrooms, a mix of shitakes, lobster, fresh porcini, chanterelle or other cultivated wild mushrooms will work here. Portobello mushrooms will turn the dish black unless you scrape the gills from the underside of the mushroom.

Spinach and Ricotta Manicotti

One 9-oz/255-g package manicotti noodles

FOR THE FILLING

3 tbsp extra-virgin olive oil

2 garlic cloves, minced

Two 10-oz/280-g packages baby spinach

Salt

Freshly ground black pepper

⅛ tsp freshly grated nutmeg

1¼ cups/325 g whole-milk ricotta

1½ cups/175 g freshly grated Parmigiano-Reggiano cheese

FOR THE CREAM SAUCE

4 tbsp/55 g unsalted butter

1 garlic clove, minced

3 tbsp all-purpose flour

1½ cups/360 ml chicken or vegetable broth

1 cup/240 ml heavy cream

1½ cups/175 g freshly grated pecorino romano cheese

Salt (optional)

4 drops Tabasco

Bright green flecks of spinach blended with ricotta peek out of the tender mani-cotti, which are bathed in a luscious creamy sauce. This is a delicious vegetarian entrée, but carnivores and vegetarians alike will be coming back for seconds! The secret to perfectly cooked pasta dishes in the slow cooker is to undercook the pasta in boiling salted water by half the recommended amount of time. That way they won't become mushy in the slow cooker.

Bring 6 qt/5.5 L of salted water to a boil. Boil the noodles for 5 minutes (or half the time suggested on the package). Drain the noodles, and separate them on a sheet of waxed paper or aluminum foil to cool.

TO MAKE THE FILLING / In a large skillet, heat the olive oil and swirl the garlic in the pan for 30 seconds, until fragrant. Add the spinach, sprinkle with salt and pep-per, add the nutmeg, and cook until the spinach is wilted and there is no more liquid in the bottom of the pan. Transfer the mixture to a food processor, and add the ricotta and Parmigiano. Pulse on and off until the mixture comes together. Transfer to a bowl. (You can store, covered, in the refrigerator for up to 3 days.)

TO MAKE THE SAUCE / In a medium saucepan, melt the butter and swirl the garlic in the pan for 30 seconds, until fragrant. Add the flour and when white bubbles appear, whisk for 2 to 3 minutes to cook the roux. Slowly add the broth and cream, and bring the sauce back to a boil, whisking constantly until thickened. Remove the pan from the heat and stir in the pecorino, whisking until the cheese is melted. Season with salt if necessary, and stir in the Tabasco. (At this point the sauce can be cooled and refrigerated for up to 4 days.)

Coat the inside of a 5- to 7-qt/4.5- to 6.5-L slow cooker with nonstick cooking spray, or line with a slow-cooker liner. Spread a layer of the sauce over the bottom of the slow cooker. Using a small offset spatula, push 2 tbsp of filling into each manicotti tube. Lay the tubes in the slow cooker, and cover with the remaining sauce. If your slow cooker is small or round, layer the tubes, alternating them with layers of the sauce. Cover the slow cooker and cook on high for 3 hours, or on low for 5 to 6 hours, until the sauce is bubbling. Remove the cover and allow the manicotti to rest for 10 minutes before serving.

Veal Manicotti

One 9-oz/255-g package manicotti noodles

FOR THE FILLING

2 tbsp unsalted butter

¼ cup/40 g finely chopped onion

Two 10-oz/280-g packages baby spinach

½ tsp freshly grated nutmeg

1½ tsp salt

½ tsp freshly ground black pepper

1½ lb/680 g ground veal

½ lb/225 g lean ground pork

1 large egg

1 cup/115 g freshly grated Parmigiano-Reggiano cheese

FOR THE SAUCE

2 tbsp extra-virgin olive oil

1 medium onion, finely chopped

1 garlic clove, minced

Pinch of red pepper flakes

Two 28- to 32-oz/800- to 910-g cans crushed tomatoes, with their juice

1 tsp salt

½ tsp freshly ground black pepper

1 cup/240 ml heavy cream

¼ cup/10 g packed fresh basil leaves, thinly sliced

2 tbsp finely chopped fresh flat-leaf parsley

1 cup/115 g freshly grated Parmigiano-Reggiano cheese

Manicotti is Italian for "little muffs." These tubes of pasta are filled with savory bits, and then covered with either a creamy béchamel or a tomato sauce. Here the manicotti are stuffed with a savory filling, and topped with a marinara cream sauce with a bit of a kick. Making dishes like this in the slow cooker helps infuse the filling and pasta with the sauce, permeating the dish.

Bring 6 qt/5.5 L of salted water to a boil. Boil the noodles for 5 minutes (or half the time suggested on the package). Drain the noodles, and separate them on a sheet of waxed paper or aluminum foil to cool.

TO MAKE THE FILLING / In a large skillet, over medium-high, heat melt the butter. Sauté the onion for 3 minutes, or until it begins to soften. Add the spinach; sprinkle with the nutmeg, salt, and pepper; and cook, turning the spinach as it wilts in the pan. When the spinach has wilted, scrape the mixture into a food processor and set aside.

Put the veal and pork in the same pan, and cook over high heat until the meats lose their pink color, stirring to break up any large clumps. Drain any excess fat or water from the meat, and transfer to the food processor. When the meat has cooled, process it and the spinach into a paste. Add the egg and cheese and process again. Or, if you don't have a food processor, use a sharp knife to mince the spinach into the meat, transfer the mixture to a bowl, and stir in the egg. (The filling can be refrigerated for up to 24 hours.)

TO MAKE THE SAUCE / In a skillet, heat the olive oil over medium-high heat, and sauté the onion, garlic, and red pepper flakes for 3 minutes, or until the onion begins to soften and the garlic is fragrant. Stir in the tomatoes, salt, and pepper and simmer for 20 minutes. Add the cream, basil, and parsley and simmer for an additional 10 minutes. (If not using immediately, cool the sauce and refrigerate, covered, for up to 3 days, or freeze for up to 2 months.)

Coat the inside of a 5- to 7-qt/4.5- to 6.5-L slow cooker with nonstick cooking spray, or line with a slow-cooker liner. Spread a thin layer of marinara cream sauce over the bottom of the slow cooker. Using a small offset spatula, push 2 tbsp of filling into each manicotti tube. Lay the tubes in the slow cooker, and cover with the remaining sauce. If your slow cooker is small or round, layer the tubes, alternating them with layers of the sauce. Sprinkle the top with the Parmigiano. Cover the slow cooker and cook on high for 3 hours, or on low for 6 hours, until the sauce is bubbling and the cheese has melted.

Uncover the slow cooker and allow the manicotti to rest for 10 minutes before serving.

Polenta

Emerging from the slow cooker creamy and smooth, without any stirring, this polenta recipe is a miracle for many cooks who love this dish. I like to serve it with sautéed greens like Swiss chard, or as a bed for beef stews or pork ragùs.

In the insert of a 4- to 6-qt/3.5- to 5.5-L slow cooker, whisk together the cornmeal, salt, broth, and milk. Cover the slow cooker and cook on high for 2 hours.

Uncover the slow cooker and stir in the butter and cheese. Re-cover the slow cooker and cook the polenta for another 45 minutes to 1 hour. Serve the polenta immediately, or keep it on the warm setting for up to 1 hour.

❖【 **VARIATION** 】❖ If you have any leftover polenta, pour it while still warm into a small square baking dish, and spread ½ in/12 mm thick. Cool the polenta, cut into squares, and sauté in olive oil until crisp on both sides. Top the polenta with bruschetta toppings like chopped tomatoes, sautéed mushrooms, or marinated artichoke hearts.

1½ cups/150 g coarsely ground cornmeal

1½ tsp salt

3 cups/720 ml chicken or vegetable broth

2½ cups/600 ml whole milk

4 tbsp/55 g unsalted butter

½ cup/60 g freshly grated Parmigiano-Reggiano cheese

Farro

2 cups/240 g farro, rinsed with cold water

4½ cups/1 L chicken or vegetable broth

Salt (optional)

Freshly ground black pepper (optional)

Farro is an ancient Roman grain that has become quite popular in recent years. A terrific source of vitamins and minerals, as well as fiber, it is also delicious. Farro has a nutty quality, similar to wild rice, but it's creamier. Serve farro as a bed for grilled meats and poultry. Store the leftover farro in the refrigerator or freezer and use it in soups, casseroles, or vegetable dishes.

Add the farro to the insert of a 4- to 6-qt/3.5- to 5.5-L slow cooker. Stir in the broth. Cover the slow cooker, and cook on high for 2 hours, or until the farro is tender.

Season with salt or pepper if necessary. Serve immediately.

Farro Risotto

Farro makes a lovely risotto with a creamy quality. Similar in preparation to traditional risotto, this dish will soon become a favorite in your house.

In a small saucepan, melt 2 tbsp of the butter over medium-high heat and sauté the shallots for 3 minutes, or until the shallots begin to soften. Add the farro, and stir to coat with the butter. Add the wine, raise the heat to high, and cook, stirring, for 3 minutes to evaporate some of the wine. Transfer the mixture to the insert of a 4- to 6-qt/3.5- to 5.5-L slow cooker and stir in the broth. Cover the slow cooker, and cook on high for 1½ hours.

Add the remaining butter and the cheese to the farro, stirring to blend. Cover the cooker, and turn the heat to low or warm. Cook for another 30 minutes, and serve the risotto immediately.

4 tbsp/55 g unsalted butter

½ cup/80 g finely chopped shallots

2 cups/240 g farro, rinsed with cold water

½ cup/120 ml dry white wine, such as Pinot Grigio or Sauvignon Blanc, or dry vermouth

4 cups/960 ml chicken or vegetable broth

¼ cup/30 g freshly grated Parmigiano-Reggiano cheese

Risotto alla Milanese

6 tbsp/85 g unsalted butter

½ cup/80 g finely chopped shallots

1 tsp saffron threads, crushed in the palm of your hand

2 cups/430 g Arborio rice

1½ cups/360 ml dry white wine, such as Pinot Grigio or Sauvignon Blanc, or dry vermouth

4 cups/960 ml chicken broth

½ cup/60 g freshly grated Parmigiano-Reggiano cheese

Salt

Freshly ground black pepper

Creamy Arborio rice becomes tender and delicious in one hour without the laborious stirring that is associated with this famous dish from the area of Emilia Romagna in Italy. Flavored with saffron, risotto alla milanese is usually served as a bed for Veal Osso Buco (page 69) or Beef in Barolo (page 62), but it is also a delicious first course.

In a small saucepan, over medium-high heat, melt 2 tbsp of the butter and sauté the shallots and saffron for 3 minutes, until the shallots are softened. Add the rice and stir until the rice is coated with the butter mixture. Raise the heat to high, add the wine, and cook, stirring, for 4 to 5 minutes, until the wine is reduced by a third. Transfer the mixture to the insert of a 4- to 6-qt/3.5- to 5.5-L slow cooker, and stir in the broth. Cover the slow cooker and cook the rice on high for 1 hour. It should be creamy and tender.

Uncover the slow cooker and stir in the remaining butter and the cheese. Season with salt and pepper. Serve the risotto immediately, or keep it on the warm setting for up to 30 minutes before serving.

Pilaf

Pilaf is a preparation that requires toasting the rice in fat—either olive oil or butter or both—and then cooking the rice in stock or broth. The flavorings vary with the region in which it is prepared: dried fruits in Morocco, onion and garlic in Greece and Turkey. Pilaf is generally served with dishes that have a rich sauce, so the pilaf will soak it up.

In a large skillet, melt the butter over medium-high heat and sauté the shallots and rice until the rice begins to toast, about 5 minutes. Transfer to the insert of a 5- to 7-qt/4.5- to 6.5-L slow cooker and stir in the broth. Cover and cook on high for 1½ to 2 hours, until the rice is tender and the liquid in the cooker is absorbed.

Uncover the slow cooker, fluff the rice, and serve.

SERVES 6 TO 8

4 tbsp/55 g unsalted butter

½ cup/50 g finely chopped shallots

3 cups/360 g long-grain rice

5 to 6 cups/1.2 to 1.4 L chicken or vegetable broth

Couscous

3 cups/720 ml chicken or vegetable broth

2 cups/400 g couscous

Couscous can be found daily on tables along the North African coast, as well as in southern Spain and France. Made from crushed durum wheat semolina, couscous is a perfect foil to absorb the juices from savory stews, and it's a terrific addition to soups, as well.

In a medium saucepan, bring the broth to a boil. Add the couscous, and stir to blend. Remove the pan from the heat, cover the saucepan, and let the couscous sit for 15 minutes. Remove the cover from the pan, and fluff the couscous with a fork. Serve immediately. Any leftover couscous can be refrigerated for up to 5 days. Couscous does not freeze well.

Simple Pita Bread

Pita bread is found in many countries along the Mediterranean, and it's really quite simple to prepare at home. The baking technique is unique; when the puffed bread comes out of the oven, it's wrapped in a clean kitchen towel to keep it soft. Flatbreads are used as a utensil to scoop up food or they can be stuffed with falafel (page 170), kebabs, meatballs (page 72) and conventional sandwich fillings. Treating your family to homemade bread is simple, and the results are terrific!

In a large mixing bowl, combine the flour, yeast, and salt, stirring to blend. Add the water and olive oil, and stir until the dough begins to come together. Turn the dough out onto a floured board and knead for 10 minutes, adding more flour as necessary when the dough becomes sticky. Coat the inside of a large bowl with a little olive oil. Transfer the dough to the bowl, turning it to coat with the oil. Cover with a kitchen towel and allow to rise for 1 hour, or until doubled in bulk. (I usually use a warmed and turned-off oven.)

Turn the dough out onto the floured board, and divide into ten equal small balls. Preheat the oven to 450°F/230°C/gas 8.

Oil a baking sheet. Roll two balls of dough into 6-in/15-cm circles and place on the prepared baking sheet. Bake for 5 minutes. The dough should puff. Bake for another 2 minutes, and remove the breads from the oven. They should be pale gold. Transfer to a platter and cover the breads with a clean kitchen towel to keep them soft. Repeat with the remaining balls of dough, two at a time, until all the flatbread has been baked. Be sure to keep the freshly baked breads wrapped in kitchen towels. Once all the bread is baked, they can be used immediately. Or you can cool them and store in zipper-top plastic bags at room temperature for up to 2 days. Or store in zipper-top freezer bags, pressing the air out, for up to 2 months in the freezer.

MAKES 10 TO 12

4½ cups/540 g bread flour, plus extra for kneading and rolling the dough

2½ tsp instant dry yeast

2 tsp salt

1⅓ cups/315 ml warm water (110°F/43°C)

3 tbsp olive oil, plus extra for the bowl and baking sheet

CH.06

VEGETABLES AND LEGUMES

Variations on the refrain "eat your veggies" are heard every night at family dinner tables in thousands of different languages around the world. In the Mediterranean region, vegetables are a greater part of the diet than meat, poultry, or seafood. Fresh vegetables in season are served at most meals in the Mediterranean.

In North Africa, conical tagines slow-cook vegetables over low heat for hours; in the northern Mediterranean, cooks stew vegetables or roast them in all manner of pots. The slow cooker can mimic this type of cooking at a low and slow simmer, to reveal beautifully flavored and brilliantly colored meatless entrées and side dishes. I love using the slow cooker in the summer to roast potatoes (see page 148), make a potato gratin (see page 149), Ratatouille (page 154), or a lovely Eggplant Moussaka (page 158) without turning on the oven and heating up the kitchen. Slow-cooked vegetables are terrific to take along to a potluck. And if you're making dinner at home, the vegetables can stay warm in the slow cooker while you prepare the rest of the meal.

When fresh vegetables are not available in the Mediterranean, or they are too costly, dried legumes are used to stretch the family food budget. Slow cookers produce the creamiest dried white beans with their slow, daylong simmer. Lentils and beans are usually served with rice, and flavored with traditional local spices.

Slow-Roasted Stuffed Tomatoes

SERVES 6

My *nonna*, Aleandra, made these tomatoes in the summertime from her incredibly delicious homegrown tomatoes and homemade bread. She would cook her version on the stove top in a covered cast-iron skillet. Like my grandmother's, these tomatoes are flavored with garlic, pecorino cheese, fresh basil, and parsley. These are terrific as a light lunch, but we love to eat them with porterhouse steaks cooked on the grill.

½ cup/120 ml extra-virgin olive oil

3 large vine-ripened tomatoes, halved

1½ tsp salt

½ tsp freshly ground black pepper

3 cups/165 g fresh bread crumbs

1½ cups/175 g freshly grated pecorino romano cheese

3 garlic cloves, minced

¼ cup/15 g finely chopped fresh basil

2 tbsp finely chopped fresh flat-leaf parsley

½ cup/120 ml chicken or vegetable broth

Pour ¼ cup/60 ml of the olive oil into the insert of a 5- to 7-qt/4.5- to 6.5-L slow cooker, and brush the sides with some of the oil. Arrange the tomato halves in the insert, cut-side up, and sprinkle with the salt and pepper.

In a small bowl, combine the bread crumbs, cheese, garlic, basil, and parsley. Mound the mixture onto each of the tomato halves (it's okay if some of it falls off onto the bottom of the insert), and drizzle with the remaining olive oil. Pour the broth into the slow cooker (but not directly over the tomatoes). Cover and cook on high for 1 hour, and baste with the pan juices.

Re-cover and cook for another 1 hour on high, until the tomatoes are tender. Allow the tomatoes to rest for 10 minutes. Serve hot or at room temperature.

VARIATION In the winter, when tomatoes are not looking or tasting so great, you can make a version with three 28- to 32-oz/800- to 910-g cans of plum tomatoes. Make the stuffing and set aside. Cut the tomatoes in half, drain, and mix with ¼ cup/60 ml extra-virgin olive oil, 5 minced garlic cloves, 2 tbsp finely chopped rosemary, 2 tsp salt, and 1 tsp pepper. Cover and cook on high for 1 hour, and sprinkle the tomatoes with the stuffing. Cover and cook for another 2 hours on high. Remove the cover, cook for another 30 minutes, uncovered, and serve.

Roasted Potatoes with Cherry Tomato Salad

3 lb/1.4 kg small Yukon gold, red-skinned, fingerling, or white creamer potatoes (see Slow Cooker Savvy)

¼ lb/115 g pancetta, coarsely chopped

8 garlic cloves, sliced

2 tsp dried oregano, or 1 tbsp finely chopped fresh rosemary (see Slow Cooker Savvy)

Salt

Freshly ground black pepper

¾ cup/180 ml extra-virgin olive oil

Grated zest of 1 lemon

2 cups/440 g cherry, grape, or pear tomatoes, halved

¼ cup/10 g packed fresh basil leaves, torn

¼ cup /60 ml red wine vinegar

I have never met a potato I didn't like. Red-skinned, russets, Peruvian purple, Yukon golds—whether creamers freshly dug out of the ground or mature, they all call my name. I could probably write a book just on the potatoes I've loved. This dish is similar to many served in southern Italy and Greece. It's flavored with garlic, lemon zest, and cured pork, which gives it a smoky flavor. I love to accompany it, on the same plate, with a cooling cherry tomato and basil salad. The potatoes and tomatoes are a light meal in themselves, but they taste great with grilled meats or seafood in the summertime.

In the insert of a 5- to 7-qt/4.5- to 6.5-L slow cooker, toss together the potatoes, pancetta, garlic, oregano, 1½ tsp salt, 1 tsp pepper, ½ cup/120 ml of the olive oil, and the lemon zest. Cover and cook on high for 3 hours, or on low for 6 hours.

In a small salad bowl, toss together the tomatoes and basil. In another bowl, whisk together the vinegar and remaining ¼ cup/60 ml olive oil. Season with salt and pepper, and pour the dressing over the tomatoes. (The tomato salad can be kept at room temperature for up to 4 hours or refrigerated for up to 24 hours. The oil in the salad may solidify, so bring the salad to room temperature about 1 hour before serving.)

When the potatoes are ready, spoon off any excess oil, and accompany each serving with some of the tomato salad.

SLOW COOKER SAVVY

I particularly like the taste and coloring of this dish when it's made with Yukon gold potatoes, but you can use any low-starch potato you have on hand.

Oregano and rosemary are two strong herbs that pair well with potatoes. But in some regions of the Mediterranean, you might find thyme, saffron, or marjoram in potato recipes, and those work well, too.

Fennel-Potato Gratin

Fragrant fennel and golden potatoes pair up in this delicious gratin filled with cheese, leeks, and a creamy sauce. Terrific to serve alongside your holiday ham, pork, or roast beef, it's equally good with grilled seafood.

~~~~~~

Coat the insert of a 5- to 7-qt/4.5- to 6.5-L slow cooker with nonstick cooking spray or line it with a slow-cooker liner. In a large skillet over medium-high heat, melt the butter with the olive oil and sauté the fennel and leeks for 5 minutes, until the leeks begin to soften. Add the salt, Tabasco, cream, and milk to the skillet, and stir to blend. Add the potatoes and cook for 6 to 8 minutes, until they are tender but not falling apart.

Remove the skillet from the heat. Spread half the potatoes in the bottom of the slow cooker. Cover with ½ cup/60 g of the Gruyère cheese. Layer the remaining potatoes on top, and sprinkle with the remaining Gruyère and the Parmigiano. Cover the slow cooker and cook on high for 3 hours, or on low for 6 hours, until the potatoes are tender and bubbling.

Allow the potatoes to rest for about 10 minutes before serving.

1 tbsp unsalted butter

2 tbsp extra-virgin olive oil

2 fennel bulbs, wispy fronds removed, thinly sliced

2 leeks (white and tender green parts), thinly sliced

1 tsp salt

½ tsp Tabasco

2 cups/480 ml heavy cream

1 cup/240 ml whole milk

1½ lb/680 g Yukon gold potatoes, thinly sliced

1½ cups/175 g shredded Gruyère cheese

½ cup/60 g finely grated Parmigiano-Reggiano cheese

Timpani of Potatoes

This is a big production, along the lines of the pasta dish served in the Stanley Tucci film *Big Night*. Like their northern counterparts, the cooks of southern Italy don't waste food, and this dish probably came about when someone had too many leftover mashed potatoes. Layered with prosciutto or salami, cheeses, garlic, and herbs, the dish bubbles away in the slow cooker, emitting aromas that will make your mouth water. Serve it directly from the slow cooker with grilled meat, poultry, or seafood, or as a luncheon main dish with fresh tomatoes from your garden, dressed with oil and lemon juice.

Boil the potatoes in salted water to cover until tender, and drain. Coat the insert of a 5- to 7-qt/4.5- to 6.5-L slow cooker with nonstick cooking spray, or line with a slow-cooker liner and brush the inside with 1 tbsp of the olive oil. Sprinkle ¼ cup/30 g of the Parmigiano over the inside of the insert, tilting to cover it with the cheese.

Combine the hot potatoes, ricotta, 1 cup/115 g Parmigiano, 1½ tsp salt, ¾ tsp pepper, 2 tbsp of the butter, the milk, and ¼ cup/15 g of the parsley in the bowl of an electric mixer. Beat until smooth. Fold in the prosciutto and artichokes, blending until well combined. Taste and adjust the salt and pepper.

Spread half the potatoes in the prepared insert, cover with half of the mozzarella, and sprinkle with ¼ cup/30 g of the remaining Parmigiano. Add the remaining potatoes and mozzarella in layers.

In a medium bowl, combine the bread crumbs, garlic, remaining Parmigiano, remaining parsley, and 2 tbsp olive oil, tossing until the crumbs are evenly moistened. Sprinkle this mixture over the mozzarella, and dot with the remaining butter. Cover the slow cooker and cook on low for 6 hours, or on high for 2½ hours, until the cheeses are melted and the casserole is bubbling.

Remove the cover from the slow cooker and allow the timpani to rest for 10 minutes before serving.

VARIATION Other meats such as, smoked ham, salami, or mortadella, can be substituted for the prosciutto. Just make sure to slice them thinly. Or, if you wish to make this vegetarian, omit the prosciutto, and fold ½ lb/225 g asparagus tips, blanched; caramelized onions; or sautéed mushrooms into the potatoes.

---

8 medium baking potatoes, peeled and cut into 1-in/2.5-cm chunks

2 to 3 tbsp olive oil

1¾ cups/175 g freshly grated Parmigiano-Reggiano cheese

½ cup/130 g ricotta cheese

Salt

Freshly ground black pepper

4 tbsp/55 g unsalted butter, softened

¼ cup/60 ml milk, or more as needed

½ cup/30 g chopped fresh flat-leaf parsley

⅓ lb/140 g thinly sliced prosciutto, large pieces of fat removed, and cut into narrow strips

One 5-to 6-oz/140- to 170-g jar marinated artichoke hearts, drained, patted dry, and quartered

1 lb/455 g fresh mozzarella cheese, sliced ¼ in/6 mm thick

¾ cup/45 g fresh bread crumbs

3 garlic cloves, minced

Potato Tagine with Lemon and Olives

¼ cup/60 ml canola oil

½ tsp saffron threads, crushed in the palm of your hand

2 tsp sweet paprika

4 garlic cloves, chopped

¼ cup/25 g finely chopped preserved lemon rind (see Slow Cooker Savvy, page 78)

1 tsp ground ginger

½ tsp ground cumin

3 lb/1.4 kg mixed medium potatoes, such as Yukon gold, purple, red-skinned, and white creamer potatoes, quartered

12 cipollini onions, peeled

1 cup/120 g picholine green olives, cracked and pitted

2 tbsp finely chopped fresh mint, for garnish

A vegetarian tagine is a superb meatless supper, or it can be served as an exotic side with roasted or grilled meats, or seafood. A good amount of aromatic spices transforms the multicolored potatoes into savory and delicious nuggets in the sauce. I love the sweetness of the cipollini onions in this dish, but if you can't find them, quarter sweet yellow onions and use them instead. You can make your own preserved lemons, or look for them in Middle Eastern markets, gourmet shops, or online (see Resources, page 184).

In the insert of a 5- to 7-qt/4.5- to 6.5-L slow cooker, combine the canola oil, saffron, paprika, garlic, preserved lemon, ginger, and cumin. Add the potatoes and onions, and stir to coat them. Cover the slow cooker and cook on high for 2 to 3 hours, or on low for 4 to 5 hours. The potatoes should be tender when pierced with the tip of a sharp knife.

Stir the olives and mint into the slow cooker. Serve the potatoes either hot or at room temperature.

Spanish Potato Tortilla

This terrific Spanish potato and onion dish, which Americans would call an omelet, makes a great quick meal, even in the slow cooker. Boil the potatoes a day or two before you plan to make it, and then surprise your family with this tortilla just an hour after assembly. Serve it with a salad and some fruit for brunch or dinner. It is best to use low-starch potatoes, such as Yukon gold or red-skinned, for this omelet. They are less likely to disintegrate while cooking.

In a large saucepan or soup pot, cook the potatoes in boiling water to cover for 20 to 30 minutes, until tender. Drain and let cool. (The potatoes can be refrigerated for up to 2 days.)

In a medium skillet, heat the olive oil over medium-high heat and sauté the onion and paprika for 3 minutes, or until the onion begins to soften. Let cool slightly. Coat the slow cooker with nonstick cooking spray or line it with a slow-cooker liner.

Peel the potatoes and slice ¼ in/6 mm thick. Spread half the potatoes in the bottom of the insert and season with salt and pepper. Spread all the onion over the potato layer. Top with the remaining potatoes, and sprinkle with salt and pepper. In a mixing bowl, whisk the eggs, season with salt and pepper, and the parsley. Pour over the potatoes and onion. Cover the slow cooker, and cook on high for 60 to 70 minutes. A knife inserted in the center of the tortilla should come out clean.

Allow the tortilla to rest, uncovered, for 10 minutes before serving.

SLOW COOKER SAVVY

When boiling potatoes, I use a pasta pentola, which is a large pot that has an insert with holes. I simply drain the potatoes in the cooking pot and transfer them to a cutting board.

8 medium Yukon gold potatoes (see Slow Cooker Savvy)

2 tbsp extra-virgin olive oil

1 medium onion, thinly sliced

1 tsp sweet paprika

Salt

Freshly ground black pepper

8 large eggs

¼ cup/15 g finely chopped fresh flat-leaf parsley

Ratatouille

2 lb/910 g purple eggplant, peeled and cut into ½-in/12-mm cubes (see Slow Cooker Savvy)

2 medium zucchini, cut into ½-in/12-mm pieces

2 medium yellow squash or yellow zucchini, cut into ½-in/12-mm pieces

4 tsp salt

¼ cup/60 ml extra-virgin olive oil

Pinch of red pepper flakes

4 garlic cloves, sliced

2 medium onions, halved and sliced crosswise into half-moons

2 tsp herbes de Provence (see Slow Cooker Savvy, page 114)

1 bay leaf

1 medium red bell pepper, cored and sliced ½ in/12 mm thick

1 medium yellow bell pepper, cored and sliced ½ in/12 mm thick

¼ cup/60 ml red wine

One 14½- to 15-oz/415- to 430-g can tomato purée

½ tsp freshly ground black pepper

Just about every home cook in the French region of Provence makes some version of ratatouille, which is made with eggplant, tomatoes, and other vegetables as well as herbs from the kitchen garden. Served as a side dish with grilled or roasted meats, poultry or seafood, ratatouille is also a lovely addition to a Frittata (page 165), omelet, or quiche. Or spoon some on a *tartine* (toast) made with good bread. Make sure you salt the eggplant and zucchini before cooking, to eliminate excess water in the finished sauce.

Put the eggplant, zucchini, and yellow squash in a colander and sprinkle with 2 tsp of the salt. Leave the vegetables in the colander for 1 hour, tossing them every 10 minutes or so. Press any excess water out of the vegetables and set aside.

In a large skillet, heat the olive oil over medium-high heat. Sauté the red pepper flakes, garlic, onions, herbes de Provence, bay leaf, and bell peppers together for about 7 minutes, until there is no liquid left in the skillet. Transfer the mixture to the insert of a 5- to 7-qt/4.5- to 6.5-L slow cooker. Stir in the eggplant and zucchini and add the wine, tomato purée, and pepper. Cover and cook on high for 2 to 3 hours, until the vegetables are tender and the sauce is thickened.

Uncover the slow cooker, discard the bay leaf, and cook on low for 30 minutes more. Serve the ratatouille hot, warm, or at room temperature. (Ratatouille will keep, covered, in the refrigerator for up to 1 week.)

SLOW COOKER SAVVY

Japanese eggplants are smaller and usually a bit more tender than common globe eggplants. If you use Japanese eggplant, you will not have to remove the skin; it is tender, and will cook down.

Peperonata

2 tbsp extra-virgin olive oil

4 large sweet yellow onions, such as Vidalia, thinly sliced

2 medium yellow bell peppers, cored and thinly sliced

2 medium orange bell peppers, cored and thinly sliced

2 medium red bell peppers, cored and thinly sliced

1 medium green bell pepper, cored and thinly sliced

2 tsp dried oregano

2 tbsp sugar

1½ tsp salt

1 tsp freshly ground black pepper

¼ cup/60 ml tomato paste

½ cup/120 ml chicken or vegetable broth

¼ cup/15 g finely chopped fresh flat-leaf parsley

Peperonata is a mélange of colorful bell peppers, onions, herbs, and tomato, which simmer and meld together in the slow cooker. It's terrific in sandwiches and over grilled entrées, burgers, and sausages. Peperonata is also great as an antipasto with crusty bread and shaved pecorino romano cheese.

In a large skillet, heat the olive oil over medium-high heat, and sauté the onions, bell peppers, oregano, sugar, salt, and black pepper for 3 minutes, or until the onions begin to soften. This may look like a mountain of onions and peppers, but it will cook down quickly. Transfer to the insert of a 5- to 7-qt/4.5- to 6.5-L slow cooker, add the tomato paste, broth, and parsley and stir to combine. Cover and cook on high for 2½ hours, or on low for 5 hours, until the peppers and onions are soft and tender.

At the end of the cooking time, uncover the slow cooker and cook for another 30 minutes. The peperonata can be served hot, cold, or at room temperature. (It will keep, covered, in the refrigerator for up to 4 days.)

SLOW COOKER SAVVY

Uncovering the slow cooker allows any excess water that may have accumulated in the sauce to evaporate. This is particularly true when vegetables contain a lot of water, like eggplant, peppers, and onions.

Briami

The summer bounty from Greek and Turkish vegetable gardens goes into an ovenproof dish to roast along with garlic, basil, and chunks of kefalotyri or Parmigiano cheese, for a knockout side dish to serve with anything from your grill. The best news is that you don't have to turn on your oven. Just pile everything into the slow cooker, set it, and forget it. You may find your family, lured by the delicious aromas, standing around the pot, waiting for the dish to finish cooking. *Briami* is usually served at room temperature, but you can also serve it warm directly from the slow cooker. Any leftovers are terrific tossed with pasta or eggs for a vegetarian main course.

Coat the inside of a 5- to 7-qt/4.5- to 6.5-L slow cooker with nonstick cooking spray, or line with a slow-cooker liner. In a medium bowl, whisk together the olive oil, garlic, red pepper flakes, salt, pepper, basil, and oregano. Drizzle a bit into the bottom of the slow cooker and lay the potatoes on top. Strew about a quarter of the onions on top of the potatoes, layer with about a third of the tomatoes, and sprinkle with half of the cheese. Arrange the zucchini over the tomatoes, and drizzle with some of the oil. Arrange another quarter of the onions on top of the zucchini, and cover the onions with another third of the tomatoes. Drizzle with oil, layer with another quarter of the onions, and cover with all of the eggplant. Layer the remaining onion and tomatoes over the eggplant, and sprinkle with the remaining cheese. Pour the rest of the oil over the top layer, and do the same with the broth. Cover and cook for 2 hours on high, or 4 hours on low.

Uncover the slow cooker, sprinkle the parsley over the top, and allow the dish to rest for about 20 minutes before serving.

SLOW COOKER SAVVY

To peel the potato or not to peel? If the skins are pristine, there is no need to remove them. In fact, many nutritional experts say most of the good stuff is in the skin. But if the skin has a greenish tinge, then do peel the potatoes. The color is from the potato's exposure to light, which can result in a toxin called solanine. The solanine may give you a stomachache.

½ cup/120 ml extra-virgin olive oil

6 garlic cloves, minced

Pinch of red pepper flakes

1½ tsp salt

½ tsp freshly ground black pepper

1 cup/45 g packed fresh basil leaves, thinly sliced

2 tsp chopped fresh Greek or Italian oregano

3 large Yukon gold, red-skinned, or white creamer potatoes (about 1½ lb/680 g total), thinly sliced (peeled or not; see Slow Cooker Savvy)

2 medium red onions, thinly sliced

4 medium vine-ripened tomatoes, cored and thinly sliced (about 1 lb/455 g total)

1 cup/115 g shredded Parmigiano-Reggiano or kefalotyri cheese

3 medium zucchini, cut into ½-in/12-mm dice

2 small Japanese eggplants, cut into ½-in/12-mm dice

¼ cup/60 ml chicken or vegetable broth

¼ cup/15 g finely chopped fresh flat-leaf parsley, for garnish

Eggplant Moussaka

A savory dish made with layers of eggplant and sometimes meat, moussaka is topped with a creamy cheese sauce, and baked until bubbling. It is a classic dish from the Greek culinary tradition, but versions of it are made in Turkey, the Middle East, and in Eastern Europe, where it may include potatoes instead of eggplant. Here the eggplant and meat are combined, and then layered with a tangy béchamel sauce. This is a lovely dish to serve with roasted or grilled meats, fish, or poultry. It also makes a tasty luncheon dish, especially when accompanied by a summer salad filled with fresh tomatoes, and tossed with a red wine vinaigrette.

FOR THE EGGPLANT AND MEAT

3 large purple eggplants (about 3 lbs/1.4 kg), peeled and cut into ½-in/12-mm pieces

2 tsp salt

4 tbsp/60 ml extra-virgin olive oil

1 large onion, finely chopped

2 garlic cloves, minced

1½ lb/680 g ground lamb

1 tsp dried oregano

¼ tsp freshly grated nutmeg

½ cup/120 ml full-bodied red wine, such as Burgundy, Chianti, or Barolo

One 14½- to 15-oz/415- to 430-g can tomato purée

½ tsp freshly ground black pepper

¼ cup/15 g finely chopped fresh flat-leaf parsley

FOR THE BÉCHAMEL

4 tbsp/55 g unsalted butter

1 garlic clove, minced

3 tbsp all-purpose flour

1½ cups/360 ml chicken or vegetable broth

1 cup/240 ml heavy cream

1½ cups/175 g grated kefalotyri cheese

Salt (optional)

5 drops Tabasco

1 cup/115 g grated kefalotyri cheese

TO MAKE THE EGGPLANT AND MEAT / Put the eggplant in a colander and sprinkle with 1 tsp of the salt. Let stand for 15 minutes. In a large skillet, heat 2 tbsp of the olive oil over medium-high heat, and sauté the onion and garlic for 3 minutes, or until the onion begins to soften. Add the lamb and cook until no longer pink, stirring to break up any large clumps. Transfer the mixture to a large bowl and set aside.

Press down on the eggplant to extract any excess water. Heat the remaining 2 tbsp of olive oil in the same skillet over high heat, and sauté the eggplant with the oregano and nutmeg, until the eggplant is golden brown. Drain off any excess moisture, add the wine, and bring to a boil, scraping up any browned bits on the bottom of the pan. Stir in the tomato purée, and fold the mixture into the lamb. Season with the remaining 1 tsp of salt and the pepper, and stir in the parsley. Set aside. (The lamb mixture can be refrigerated for up to 2 days before assembling the moussaka.)

TO MAKE THE BÉCHAMEL / In a medium saucepan, melt the butter and swirl the garlic in the pan for 30 seconds, until fragrant. Add the flour and cook, whisking constantly. When white bubbles form on the surface, cook for another 2 to 3 minutes, still whisking. Slowly add the broth and cream, bring the sauce back to a boil, and cook, whisking, until thickened. Remove the pan from the heat and stir in the cheese, whisking until the cheese is melted. Season with salt if necessary, and stir in the Tabasco. (At this point the sauce can be cooled and refrigerated for up to 4 days.)

When you're ready to assemble the moussaka, line the insert of a 5- to 7-qt/ 4.5- to 6.5-L slow cooker with a slow-cooker liner, or coat with nonstick cooking spray. Spread out a third of the béchamel in the bottom of the insert. Top with half of the lamb mixture, and then half of the remaining béchamel. Layer the remaining lamb mixture over the sauce, and top with the remaining béchamel. Sprinkle with the cheese. Cover and cook on low for 5 hours; the casserole will be bubbling and the cheese will be melted.

Uncover the slow cooker and let the moussaka rest for 20 minutes in the cooker before serving.

VARIATION In some Mediterranean regions, moussaka is prepared without meat. For a vegetarian entrée, you can do the same.

Turkish Stuffed Eggplants

SERVES 6

In Turkish this dish is called *imam bayildi*, which means "the priest fainted." It is said to have been prepared by the favorite wife of an *imam*, or Turkish priest, who swooned in ecstasy. Traditionally made as a starter or *meze*, it is generally served at room temperature, but is delightful as a hot entrée, as well. The eggplant is cut in half; the inside is scored and filled with a tomato, garlic, and parsley mixture; and it bakes low and slow to keep the eggplant tender. This dish is stellar served alongside grilled lamb, beef, or seafood.

Pour ¼ cup/60 ml of the olive oil into the insert of a 5- to 7-qt/4.5- to 6.5-L slow cooker, and brush the bottom and sides with the oil. Cut each eggplant in half lengthwise (no need to remove the stem), and score the flesh every ¼ in/6 mm, being careful not to cut the skin. Arrange the eggplant, skin-side down, in the insert, and sprinkle with some salt and pepper.

In a large skillet, heat the remaining olive oil over medium-high heat, and sauté the onion and garlic for 3 minutes, or until the onion begins to soften. Add the tomatoes and parsley, season with salt and pepper, and sauté for another 5 minutes, until the liquid in the pan has almost evaporated. Using a large spoon, spoon the tomato mixture over the eggplants, covering each half with some of the mixture. Cover the slow cooker and cook on high for 2 hours, or on low for 4 hours. The eggplant feel tender when the tip of a sharp knife is inserted into the thickest part.

Uncover the slow cooker, and let the eggplant rest for 10 minutes. Then lift the eggplant out of the slow cooker with a long spatula, and transfer to a serving platter. If there is any juice in the bottom of the cooker, spoon it over the eggplant. Serve the eggplant with the toasted pita and yogurt on the side.

½ cup/120 ml extra-virgin olive oil

3 small eggplants

Salt

Freshly ground black pepper

1 large onion, finely chopped

4 garlic cloves, minced

One 14½- to 15-oz/415- to 430-g can chopped tomatoes, with their juice

¼ cup/15 g finely chopped fresh flat-leaf parsley

Six 8-in/20-cm round pita breads, quartered and toasted

1 cup/240 ml Greek-style yogurt, for serving

Braised Baby Artichokes with Dill Aioli

Sweet little baby artichokes appear in the spring, and they make a terrific side dish for any grilled or roasted entrée. You can also offer these babies as a first course. They're braised in a lemony broth and served with an aioli sauce for dipping. The sauce is delicious over asparagus and broccoli, too.

FOR THE DILL AIOLI

2 cups/480 ml mayonnaise

¼ cup/60 ml fresh lemon juice

4 garlic cloves, minced

2 tbsp finely chopped fresh dill

4 drops Tabasco

Salt

Freshly ground black pepper

FOR THE ARTICHOKES

2 large lemons, quartered

2 bay leaves

1 tsp dried thyme

2 cups/480 ml dry white wine, such as Pinot Grigio or Sauvignon Blanc, or dry vermouth

10 black peppercorns

6 garlic cloves, peeled

12 baby artichokes, stems trimmed flush with the bottom, and halved lengthwise

TO MAKE THE AIOLI / In a mixing bowl, whisk together the mayonnaise, lemon juice, garlic, dill, and Tabasco. Season with salt and pepper. Refrigerate the aioli for at least 2 hours before serving. (The aioli will keep in an airtight container in the refrigerator for up to 1 week.)

TO MAKE THE ARTICHOKES / Squeeze the lemons into the insert of a 5- to 7-qt/ 4.5- to 6.5-L slow cooker, and add the lemons to the cooker. Combine the remaining ingredients in the slow cooker. Cover and cook on low for 2 hours, until the artichokes are tender and a leaf is easily removed.

Serve the artichokes with the aioli.

SLOW COOKER SAVVY

The braising liquid can be strained and frozen for use later as a soup stock.

Stuffed Artichokes

The slow cooker is perfect for preparing and serving these luscious artichokes, and it simplifies a recipe that has scared off many a home cook. A garlicky bread stuffing with sausage and a hint of lemon is stuffed into the outer leaves. The result is a terrific first course or side dish.

½ cup/120 ml extra-virgin olive oil

1½ cups/360 ml dry white wine, such as Pinot Grigio or Sauvignon Blanc, or dry vermouth

6 garlic cloves; 2 peeled, 4 minced

6 black peppercorns

Juice of 1 lemon

6 large globe artichokes, stems trimmed flush with the bottom and tough outer leaves removed

½ lb/225 g sweet Italian sausages, removed from their casings

4 cups/220 g fresh bread crumbs

½ cup/60 g freshly grated Parmigiano-Reggiano cheese

1½ cups/175 g freshly grated pecorino romano cheese

Grated zest of 1 lemon

¼ cup/15 g finely chopped fresh basil

¼ cup/15 g finely chopped fresh flat-leaf parsley

1 tsp freshly ground black pepper

In the insert of a 5- to 7-qt/4.5- to 6.5-L slow cooker, combine ¼ cup/60 ml of the olive oil, the wine, peeled garlic, peppercorns, and lemon juice. Using your fingers, loosen the artichoke leaves, so that there are spaces between them.

In a small sauté pan, cook the sausage until it is no longer pink, breaking up any large clumps. Drain the sausage, transfer to a mixing bowl, and allow to cool slightly. Add the bread crumbs, both cheeses, minced garlic, lemon zest, basil, parsley, and pepper to the sausage and stir to combine.

Using a spoon, push the stuffing into the spaces between the artichoke leaves. The artichokes will begin to get fatter as you put in more stuffing. Arrange them in the slow cooker and drizzle with the remaining olive oil. Cover and cook on low for 5 hours, until a leaf will release easily and the artichoke heart feels tender when pierced with the tip of a sharp knife.

Serve the artichokes hot or at room temperature.

Frittata

This savory egg dish is one of my favorites, with salty prosciutto and elegant artichoke hearts mingling with the eggs and a bit of pecorino romano cheese. Serve this for a light supper or brunch with a fruit salad and a crisp white wine, like Pinot Grigio.

~~~~~~

In a medium skillet, heat the olive oil over medium-high heat and sauté the shallots and artichoke hearts for 5 to 6 minutes, until the shallots are softened and any liquid in the pan has evaporated. Season the mixture with the salt and pepper and allow to cool.

Coat the inside of a 5- to 7-qt/4.5- to 6.5-L slow cooker with nonstick cooking spray, or line the insert with a slow-cooker liner. In a large bowl, whisk together the eggs until combined. Stir in the prosciutto, cheese, and the reserved artichoke mixture and pour into the insert. Cover and cook on high for 60 to 70 minutes, until a knife inserted into the center of the frittata comes out clean.

Uncover the slow cooker and allow the frittata to rest for 10 minutes in the cooker before serving.

~~~~~~

VARIATION Frittate are a terrific way to use up leftover veggies and pasta. In Italy you will find leftover pasta in many frittate, along with cheeses and meats. Instead of artichokes, substitute the same quantity of cooked vegetables, such as zucchini, asparagus, chard, kale, corn, or broccoli. To make a pasta frittata, substitute 6 oz/170 g of cooked pasta for the artichokes. If you like, you can also replace the prosciutto with ⅓ to ½ lb/140 to 225 g of bite-size pieces of cooked meat, poultry, or fish. And feel free to substitute your favorite cheese for the pecorino, too.

---

2 tbsp extra-virgin olive oil

2 medium shallots, finely chopped

One 10-oz/280-g package frozen artichoke hearts, defrosted and coarsely chopped

1 tsp salt

½ tsp freshly ground black pepper

10 large eggs

8 thin slices prosciutto, finely chopped

⅔ cup/75 g freshly grated Pecorino Romano cheese

Portuguese Sausage and Eggs

Spicy Portuguese sausage cooks in a saffron-scented tomato sauce for a few hours, and then eggs are poached on the top of the sauce. This is a terrific light supper, or a great dish to serve for brunch.

In a large skillet over medium-high heat, cook the linguiça to render its fat, about 5 minutes. Add the onion, garlic, bell pepper, and saffron and sauté for 3 minutes, or until the onion begins to soften. Stir in the tomatoes, and transfer the contents of the pan to the insert of a 5- to 7-qt/4.5- to 6.5-L slow cooker. Stir in the broth. Cover and cook on high for 2 hours, or on low for 3 to 4 hours.

Stir the peas into the sauce, and break the eggs on top, so that they rest on the surface of the sauce. Sprinkle the eggs with salt, pepper, and the parsley. Cover and cook on high for 35 to 45 minutes. The eggs will be set, but runny in the middle. If you prefer your eggs cooked through, increase the time for the eggs to 55 to 65 minutes on high.

Using a large serving spoon, ladle the eggs and some of the sauce onto plates. Serve immediately.

1 lb/455 g linguiça or another smoked sausage, cut into ½-in/12-mm rounds

1 large onion, finely chopped

1 garlic clove, minced

1 medium red bell pepper, cored and finely chopped

1 tsp saffron threads, crushed in the palm of your hand

One 14½- to 15-oz/415- to 430-g can chopped tomatoes, with their juice

1 cup/240 ml chicken broth

2 cups/340 g frozen petite peas, defrosted

8 large eggs

Salt

Freshly ground black pepper

½ cup/30 g finely chopped fresh flat-leaf parsley

Braised Green Beans,
Tomatoes, Feta, and Mint

2 tbsp extra-virgin olive oil

6 garlic cloves, minced

2 medium shallots, finely chopped

½ tsp dried oregano

One 28- to 32-oz/800- to 910-g can chopped tomatoes, with their juice

1 cup/240 ml chicken or vegetable broth

1½ lb/680 g green beans, ends trimmed, and cut into 1-in/2.5-cm pieces

3 tbsp thinly sliced fresh mint leaves

Salt

Freshly ground black pepper

1 cup/60 g crumbled feta cheese, for garnish

Bright red tomatoes and garlicky green beans combine in your slow cooker to make a tasty side dish that is terrific served alongside grilled meats or seafood.

In a large skillet, heat the olive oil over medium-high heat and sauté the garlic and shallots for 3 minutes, or until the shallots begin to soften. Add the oregano and tomatoes, and stir to combine. Transfer the mixture to the insert of a 5- to 7-qt/4.5- to 6.5-L slow cooker. Stir in the broth and green beans. Cover and cook on high for 2 hours, or on low for 4 hours.

Sprinkle the beans with the mint and season with salt and pepper. Serve hot or at room temperature, garnished with the feta cheese.

SLOW COOKER SAVVY

I am not a fan of dried mint, and prefer to let oregano flavor the beans and tomatoes while they cook. The finish of fresh mint leaves gives the dish a bright touch.

Egyptian Lentils and Rice

This is definitely comfort food for the Egyptian soul. There are more recipes for this dish, called *kushari* in Arabic, than I can count. The recipe is basically caramelized onions, stewed lentils, and rice topped with a garlicky tomato sauce. In many homes it is a four-pot meal: one for each of the elements in the dish. But with your slow cooker, you can have the onions, lentils, and tomato sauce simmering. Just pop the rice into your rice cooker and you have a satisfying, inexpensive meal any night of the week. Serve this with pita bread and a dollop of Greek-style yogurt for a real treat!

In a large skillet over medium-high heat, melt the butter with the olive oil. Stir in the onions, cayenne, salt, and sugar and cook until the onions become translucent. Add the garlic and cook until the onions begin to turn golden brown, then add the tomatoes.

Transfer the mixture to the insert of a 5- to 7-qt/4.5- to 6.5-L slow cooker. Stir in the lentils and the broth. Cover and cook for 7 to 8 hours on low, until the lentils are tender.

Uncover the slow cooker and skim off any excess fat from the top of the lentils. Serve the lentils over rice.

2 tbsp unsalted butter

2 tbsp extra-virgin olive oil

4 large sweet yellow onions, such as Vidalia, coarsely chopped

Pinch of cayenne pepper

2 tsp salt

1 tbsp sugar

6 garlic cloves, sliced

Two 28- to 32-oz/800- to 910-g cans tomato purée

1 cup/200 g brown lentils, rinsed and picked over for stones and grit

3 cups/720 ml chicken or vegetable broth

Cooked rice, for serving

Falafel in Saffron Tomato Sauce

Falafel, a popular street food in the Middle East and North Africa, is usually deep-fried and tucked into pita with a salad of lettuce and tomatoes. This dish is a little bit of a riff on the original chickpea balls. They're sautéed in olive oil, and then dropped into a savory saffron tomato sauce to simmer and soak up all the flavor. Serve the falafel over couscous, or wrapped in pita (see page 143) with a topping of yogurt to cool the spicy sauce.

FOR THE SAUCE

2 tbsp extra-virgin olive oil

1 medium onion, finely chopped

2 garlic cloves, minced

Pinch of red pepper flakes

1 tsp saffron threads, crushed in the palm of your hand

Two 28- to 32-oz/800- to 910-g cans chopped tomatoes, with their juice

1 cup/240 ml chicken or vegetable broth

FOR THE FALAFEL

Two 14½- to 15-oz/415- to 430-g cans chickpeas, rinsed and drained

2 medium shallots, quartered

3 garlic cloves, peeled

1 tsp ground cumin

½ tsp ground coriander

1 tbsp fresh lemon juice

¼ cup/15 g finely chopped fresh cilantro

¼ cup/15 g finely chopped fresh flat-leaf parsley

1 cup/240 ml extra-virgin olive oil

1 cup/130 g all-purpose flour

¼ cup/15 g finely chopped fresh flat-leaf parsley

Salt (optional)

Freshly ground black pepper (optional)

TO MAKE THE SAUCE / In a large skillet, heat the olive oil over medium-high heat and sauté the onion, garlic, red pepper flakes, and saffron for 3 minutes, or until the onion begins to soften. Add the tomatoes and bring to a boil. Transfer the mixture to the insert of a 5- to 7-qt/4.5- to 6.5-L slow cooker and stir in the broth. Cover the slow cooker and set it on high while making the falafel.

TO MAKE THE FALAFEL / In a food processor, combine the chickpeas, shallots, garlic, cumin, coriander, and lemon juice. Pulse on and off to break up the shallots, and then process for 30 seconds, until the mixture is puréed. Transfer the chickpea mixture to a mixing bowl, and stir in the cilantro, parsley, and 2 tbsp of the olive oil. Form the mixture into 1-in/2.5-cm balls. Put the flour in a shallow dish, and roll the falafel in the flour. Heat the remaining olive oil over high heat, and cook the balls, a few at a time, being careful not to crowd the pan, until the balls are crisp all over.

Drain the falafel on paper towels and transfer to the sauce in the slow cooker. Cook the falafel on high for 2 hours, or on low for 4 hours.

Stir the parsley into the sauce, taste for seasoning, and adjust with salt or pepper if needed. Serve immediately.

Pancetta and Rosemary Beans

A change of pace from the plain beans in the usual preparation, these are flavored with pancetta, which is an Italian bacon, and rosemary. This is a typical dish in the Umbrian and Tuscan countryside.

Wash the beans in cold water, picking them over for any broken beans or stones. Put the beans in a large bowl and add enough cold water to cover them by about 2 in/5 cm. Cover with plastic wrap and let stand overnight.

In a medium skillet, heat the olive oil over medium-high heat and cook the pancetta until crisp. Add the garlic and rosemary and cook for another 2 minutes, until the oil is fragrant.

Rinse the beans and put them in the slow cooker. Add the contents of the skillet to the slow cooker, and stir in the broth. Cover and cook on low for 8 to 9 hours, until the beans are tender.

Season the beans with salt and pepper and serve.

1 lb/455 g dried small white beans

¼ cup/60 ml extra-virgin olive oil

4 thin slices pancetta, finely diced

2 garlic cloves, sliced

2 tsp finely chopped fresh rosemary

6 cups/1.4 L chicken or vegetable broth

Salt

Freshly ground black pepper

White Beans in the Slow Cooker

1 lb/455 g small white beans

6 cups/1.4 L chicken or vegetable broth

Salt

Freshly ground black pepper

Small white beans and larger cannellini are a part of Mediterranean cuisine that can't be ignored. A pot of white beans is left simmering on many stove tops in the regions, to cook into creamy goodness and serve as part of the meal. The slow cooker is the perfect vessel to cook these beans over a long, leisurely period of time. The result is a creamy pot of beans to flavor any way you would like. Serve the beans as a side dish or as a bed for grilled or slow-cooked meats and vegetables.

Wash the beans in cold water, picking them over for any broken beans or stones. Put the beans in a large bowl and add enough cold water to cover them by about 2 in/5 cm. Cover with plastic wrap and let stand overnight.

Rinse the beans and put them into the insert of a 5- to 7-qt/4.5- to 6.5-L slow cooker. Add the broth, cover, and cook on low for 8 to 9 hours, until the beans are tender.

Season the beans with salt and pepper. Serve immediately, or keep the beans on the warm setting for up to 6 hours.

SLOW COOKER SAVVY

Always salt the beans after cooking. Adding salt to the slow cooker can toughen the skin of the beans.

If you are cooking cannellini beans (large white beans), they will need from 10 to 12 hours on low.

White Beans Smothered with Tomatoes and Garlic

SERVES 6 TO 8

Creamy, spicy, and tender, this white bean dish is a perfect complement to any grilled entrée, or it can be served as a vegetarian entrée. This type of bean dish is served in the central and southern regions of Italy, and in areas of France and North Africa, with regional seasonings: wild oregano in Sicily, herbes de Provence in France, and harissa in North Africa.

Wash the beans in cold water, picking them over for any broken beans or stones. Put the beans in a large bowl, and add enough cold water to cover them by about 2 in/5 cm. Cover with plastic wrap and let stand overnight.

In a large skillet, heat the olive oil over medium-high heat and sauté the garlic, onion, and sage for 3 minutes, or until the onion begins to soften. Add the tomatoes, bring to a boil, and scrape up any browned bits on the bottom of the pan.

Rinse the beans and put them in the slow cooker. Transfer the contents of the skillet to the slow cooker insert, and stir in the broth. Cook on low for 8 to 9 hours, until the beans are tender.

Season the beans with salt and pepper and serve.

1 lb/455 g dried small white beans

2 tbsp extra-virgin olive oil

6 garlic cloves, sliced

1 large sweet yellow onion, such as Vidalia, finely chopped

2 tsp dried sage (not rubbed)

One 28- to 32-oz/800- to 910-g can chopped tomatoes, with their juice

6 cups/1.4 L chicken or vegetable broth

Salt

Freshly ground black pepper

CH.07

SAUCES AND CONDIMENTS

❦

Sauces and condiments are a nice backup for you to have in your culinary repertoire. They add color, texture, spice, and zest to many dishes. And the slow cooker cooks them low and slow in large quantities, so that you can save some for another day. Most can be refrigerated for a few days, others can actually be frozen and kept on hand for emergencies. Best of all, when served alongside your Mediterranean dishes, they bring the flavors together, balancing sweet, salty, tart, and smoky.

Basic Marinara Sauce

¼ cup/60 ml extra-virgin olive oil

2 medium onions, finely chopped

4 garlic cloves, minced

Pinch of red pepper flakes

Four 28- to 32-oz/800- to 910-g cans crushed tomatoes, with their juice

Salt

Freshly ground black pepper

½ cup/20 g packed fresh basil leaves, thinly sliced

¼ cup/15 g finely chopped fresh flat-leaf parsley

A basic tomato sauce is part of the Mediterranean diet. Whether you're serving it with pasta or adding it to a dish, this sauce will get you where you need to go. You can freeze the sauce in 1- or 2-cup/240- or 480-ml portions, to quickly defrost when you need it. A marinara is the basis for many different sauces, like Bolognese (page 75) or Beef Pizzaiola (page 61). It's a great basic to have in your repertoire, and so easy to produce in the slow cooker.

Heat the olive oil in a large skillet over medium-high heat, and sauté the onions, garlic, and red pepper flakes for 3 minutes, or until the onions begin to soften and the garlic is fragrant. Transfer the mixture to the insert of a 4- to 6-qt/3.5- to 5.5-L slow cooker, and stir in the tomatoes, 2 tsp salt, and 1 tsp pepper. Cover and cook on high for 4 hours, or on low for 8 to 9 hours.

At the end of the cooking time, stir in the basil and parsley, and season with salt and pepper. If you are not using the sauce immediately, allow it to cool to room temperature and store in airtight containers in the refrigerator for up to 5 days, or freeze for up to 6 months.

VARIATIONS Although marinara is traditionally made in Italy, it is a basic sauce that is easily adaptable to the flavors of other Mediterranean regions. For a North African flavor, replace the basil with chopped cilantro. Or replace the basil with fresh thyme or tarragon for a sauce with French notes. For a Spanish sauce, stick with the parsley, and for a Greek touch, replace the basil with oregano.

Caponata

A relish or side dish to serve warm or cold with grilled entrées, caponata is said to have originated in Sicily. But you will find versions of it all around the southern Mediterranean. Sweet, spicy, and salty, it's great for serving with crostini, or for topping grilled fish or chicken. I have also been known to toss it with penne or shell pasta for a pasta course.

In a large skillet, heat the olive oil over medium-high heat. Add the onion, garlic, and celery and sauté for about 3 minutes, until the onion begins to soften. Transfer the mixture to the insert of a 5- to 7-qt/4.5- to 6.5-L slow cooker. Add the eggplant, bell peppers, oregano, salt, and red pepper flakes to the skillet and sauté over medium-high heat until the eggplant begins to soften, 4 to 5 minutes. Add the vinegar and cook until it evaporates a bit. Add the tomatoes and raisins, and stir together. Transfer the contents of the skillet to the slow cooker. Cover and cook on low for 5 hours.

Add the capers, olives, and parsley to the slow cooker and cook for another 1 hour, until the eggplant is tender. Remove the caponata from the slow cooker and serve warm, cold, or at room temperature. Caponata will keep in the refrigerator, covered, for up to 1 week.

2 tbsp extra-virgin olive oil

1 sweet yellow onion, such as Vidalia, finely chopped

4 garlic cloves, minced

4 ribs celery, finely chopped

2 medium purple eggplants, finely diced

1 medium red bell pepper, cored and cut into ½-in/12-mm pieces

1 medium yellow bell pepper, cored and cut into ½-in/12-mm pieces

2 tsp dried oregano

1 tsp salt

Pinch of red pepper flakes

½ cup/120 ml balsamic vinegar

One 14½- to 15-oz/415- to 430-g can chopped tomatoes, drained

1½ cups/255 g golden raisins

⅓ cup/30 g capers packed in brine, drained

½ cup/50 g pitted kalamata or your favorite olives

½ cup/30 g finely chopped fresh flat-leaf parsley

Roasted Garlic

4 cups/960 ml good-quality extra-virgin olive oil

2 cups/200 g peeled garlic cloves (about 6 heads; see Slow Cooker Savvy)

I'm indebted to my friends Allison and Dane Millner, owners of Sierra Subs and Salads in Three Rivers, California, for this brilliant idea. Both are terrific cooks, and their little shop turns out some of the best food in the area. This roasted garlic is one of the secrets of their famous baked potato soup. It yields lots of garlic. Use it to flavor dishes, spread it on bruschetta, and make garlic butter. The garlic-flavored oil can be used when you need a garlic flavor as the base for your dishes. Although the garlic is perishable, the oil will keep in the fridge for months.

Pour the olive oil into the slow cooker, and add the garlic. Cover and cook on high for 2 hours, until the garlic is tender.

Remove the garlic from the oil, and mash with a fork. Cover and refrigerate for up to 3 days. (Garlic doesn't freeze well.) Strain the oil into a jar with an airtight cover, and refrigerate for up to 6 months. Makes about 3¾ cups/890 ml garlic oil.

SLOW COOKER SAVVY

I usually don't recommend using the peeled garlic you find in the supermarket, but for this recipe, it is a great time-saver.

Balsamic Caramelized Onions

These sweet and tart onions are a wonderful *condimento* to serve with bruschetta, or with grilled meats, poultry, or pork. The slow cooker cooks down the onions until they almost melt into the sweet and tart sauce. I love to serve these with a soft chèvre on toasted baguettes.

Divide the butter between two large skillets and melt it over medium-high heat. Add half the onions to each skillet and sauté for 3 to 4 minutes to soften them. (Or sauté the onions in one pan in batches.) Transfer the onions to the insert of a 4- to 6-qt/3.5- to 5.5-L slow cooker, stir in the brown sugar and vinegar, and toss to coat. Cover the slow cooker and cook on high for 4 hours, or on low for 8 hours. The onions should be softened, and the sauce should be thickened.

Cool the onions and sauce to room temperature; the sauce will thicken as it cools. Cover and refrigerate for up to 2 months.

MAKES ABOUT 5 CUPS/1.2 L

½ cup/115 g unsalted butter

6 large sweet yellow onions, such as Vidalia, coarsely chopped

1 cup/200 g firmly packed dark brown sugar

1½ cups/360 ml balsamic vinegar

½ cup/30 g finely chopped fresh flat-leaf parsley

Périgord Fig and Onion Jam

½ cup/115 g unsalted butter

6 large sweet yellow onions, such as Vidalia, coarsely chopped

1 cup/200 g firmly packed brown sugar

1½ cups/360 g balsamic vinegar

24 dried figs, coarsely chopped

I can't count the number of times I have shared this recipe with friends; it is the quintessential melding of sweet, tart, and savory. Although it is customarily made with prunes in the Dordogne area of France, I find that Americans prefer to use dried figs or a combination of figs and prunes. This jam is traditionally served with seared foie gras, but I love to use it with creamy goat cheese or other cheeses on toasted slices of baguette. The jam is also delicious to add to the slow cooker when cooking pork. The savory juices are great served over buttered noodles.

Divide the butter between two large skillets and melt it over medium-high heat. Add half the onions to each skillet and sauté for 3 to 4 minutes to soften them. (Or sauté the onions in one pan in batches.) Transfer the onions to the insert of a 4- to 6-qt/3.5- to 5.5-L slow cooker; stir in the brown sugar, vinegar, and figs; and toss to coat. Cover the slow cooker and cook on high for 4 hours, or on low for 8 hours. The onions and figs should be softened, and the sauce should be thickened.

Cool mixture to room temperature; the sauce will thicken as it cools. Cover and refrigerate for up to 2 months.

Oranges Poached in Port and Honey

Ruby port from Portugal and oranges from Spain are a match made in culinary heaven, especially when simmered with honey, cloves, and allspice. This dish can be served as a dessert, or as a side dish with pork or poultry.

SERVES 6 TO 8

8 large oranges

2 cups/480 ml ruby port

1 cup/240 ml honey

2 whole cloves

2 tsp whole allspice berries

Cut off the ends of the oranges to expose the fruit. To remove the peel, stand each orange on a cutting board, and using a flexible knife, such as a boning knife, cut away the peel and pith, following the contour of the fruit. Continue around the orange in this way, until the all the peel and pith are removed. Once the oranges have been peeled, slice them crosswise ½ in/12 mm thick.

Arrange the oranges in the insert of a 4- to 6-qt/3.5- to 5.5-L slow cooker. In a large measuring cup, whisk together the port and honey and pour over the oranges. Add the cloves and allspice berries to the cooker. Cover and cook on high for 1½ hours, or on low for 3 hours.

Carefully remove the oranges with a slotted spoon and transfer them to a serving platter. Strain the sauce into a saucepan, bring to a boil, and continue boiling to reduce the sauce by half. It will be quite syrupy and coat the back of a spoon. Cool slightly, and serve over the oranges. The oranges will keep, covered, in the refrigerator for up to 3 days, and the sauce can be frozen for up to 4 months.

SLOW COOKER SAVVY

I have served these oranges with a potato tortilla and a vegetable frittata to rave reviews. I make them the day before so that the slow cooker is available to cook the frittata for brunch.

Pears in Honey and Muscat

Poached pears make a terrific ending to any meal, but they can also be served as a side dish or garnish, which is especially tasty when the pears are flavored with this exotic mix of honey, sweet Muscat wine, and cinnamon sticks. Muscat grapes are thought to be the oldest known domesticated grapes in the world. They are found throughout the Mediterranean region, where some countries use the grapes for sparkling wines (Muscat d'Asti in Italy) or fortified wines (sherries in Spain and Portugal), and as table grapes (North African countries).

Muscat wine is generally sweet, almost like a syrup. When it's combined with honey, spices, and pears in the slow cooker, the whole is even more delicious than its parts. Try serving the pears with a dollop of Greek-style yogurt in the center, and drizzle the sauce over the yogurt. Or serve the pears filled with vanilla gelato, and spoon the warm sauce over them.

Pour the wine and honey into the insert of a 4- to 6-qt/3.5- to 5.5-L slow cooker. Whisk to blend the honey into the wine. Add the cinnamon sticks and cloves, and put the pears into the slow cooker, wedging them to fit. You may have to stack them. Spoon some of the wine mixture over the pears. Cover the slow cooker and cook on high for 1 hour, or on low for 2 hours, until the pears are softened.

Carefully lift the pears out of the slow cooker using a slotted spoon, and transfer them to a serving platter. Strain the sauce into a saucepan, bring the sauce to a boil, and continue boiling until reduced by half. It should be quite syrupy and coat the back of a spoon.

Serve the pears warm with some of the sauce spooned over them. The pears can be refrigerated, covered, for up to 2 days. The sauce can be frozen for up to 4 months.

SLOW COOKER SAVVY

I'm always asked how many pear halves to serve to guests. For this dish, I would say one half per person is a nice portion, but it will depend upon what else is served and whether this is dessert or a side dish. You may end up with a few extra halves, but they won't be around long, trust me!

SERVES 6 TO 8

2 cups/480 ml Muscat wine

½ cup/240 ml honey

Three 3-in/7.5-cm cinnamon sticks

2 whole cloves

4 firm large red pears, cored and halved

Resources

D'ARTAGNAN

www.dartagnan.com
Duck, duck fat, sausages, and truffle oils

JOIE DE VIVRE

www.frenchselections.com
Merguez sausages and French sausages, duck
and duck fat, and all things French

LA TIENDA

www.tienda.com
Spanish ingredients and cookware, including
a great selection of Serrano ham and paella pans

PENZEYS SPICES

www.penzeys.com
Just about any spice you can think of,
from Aleppo pepper to zatar

THE SPICE HOUSE

www.thespicehouse.com
Another great source for spices and spice blends

ZAMOURI SPICES

www.zamourispices.com
Preserved lemons and all things Moroccan,
including spices, olives, and oils

GENERAL COOKING EQUIPMENT

www.discountcooking.com
www.amazon.com
www.kitchenshoppe.com
www.cookswaresonline.com
www.k-art.com

Index